To Dream of Freedom

Roy Clews

The story of MAC and the Free Wales Army

y Lolfa

First edition: 1980
Second revised edition: 2001
Third edition: 2004

Cover: Ceri Jones

ISBN: 0 86243 586 2

Printed, published and bound in Wales
using acid-free and partly recycled paper
by Y Lolfa Cyf., Talybont, Ceredigion, SY24 5AP
e-mail ylolfa@ylolfa.com
internet www.ylolfa.com
phone (01970) 832 304
fax 832 782
isdn 832813

This is the true account of a rebellion against the British Crown.

It took place in Wales during the 1960's, and apart from those who died bloodily many of the leading protagonists are today still in Wales.

Many of the bombing incidents described are even yet unsolved, and no one has ever been charged and convicted concerning them. For this reason certain names have been withheld in this account, and some anonymity has been respected.

THANKS

The publishers wish to acknowledge their debt to the *Western Mail* for the many press cuttings etc. which they have used in this book, and in particular, for the map on p.216 which is also reproduced on the back cover. The publishers also wish to thank Denis Coslett and the National Library of Wales for the extra photographs that appear in this new updated edition.

Foreword

WHEN I WAS ASKED TO WRITE A FOREWORD to this second edition of *To Dream of Freedom*, I experienced a surge of widely differing emotions, pride, grief, nostalgia, anger, humility, because my father, Julian Cayo-Evans, was one of the leaders of the Free Wales Army. An organisation much reviled by the British Ruling Establishment. Maybe because it sent a frisson of fear shivering through their arrogant, smug complacency.

I was only a child when my father and his comrades challenged the rule of the 'British Establishment' over our ancient country of Wales. My father was an exciting and colourful personality. Handsome, articulate, passionate, well-educated, he shone brightly in the newspapers, the magazines and on the TV screen. Some of my earliest memories are of my father asking:

'Are we not a Country? A Welsh Nation? Why should we not govern ourselves? Why should we not police our own streets? Have our own Welsh Army? Produce and accept our own Welsh Royalty?'

As that small Welsh child, I was enthralled by the impassioned rhetoric, and thrilled by the defiant men who so proudly wore the green-peaked caps and uniforms of the Free Wales Army.

Now as an adult, hopefully having gained some insight and wisdom as a result of my own personal Calvary, I am immensely proud that my father stood shoulder to shoulder with such gallant Welsh patriots as Denis Coslett of the Free

Wales Army, John Barnard Jenkins, the commander of the Mudiad Amddifyn Cymru, and others too numerous to list in this short introduction.

The usual accusations levied against the Free Wales Army, and the Mudiad Amddiffyn Cymru, are that…

They were seditious!
They were anti-royalist!
They were Welsh Republican!
They were anti-democratic!

I would answer… "YES" to all these charges.

Then I would ask the reader to look at the reality of Wales today? What does our charade of democracy mean to the average person in the street? What does it mean to all those men and women who have lost their reason for being. Who have lost their dignity as wage earners, as supporters of their families. The mines, the steelworks, the farms, the dairies, the clothing factories, the high-tech industries are closing daily. Tens of thousands of Welshmen and Welshwomen are being ejected into unemployment. Violent crime is ever increasing and is now at an all-time high. Corruption in both national and local government is becoming ever more disturbingly apparent. Decent people are fast losing all confidence in the willingness of their political rulers to enforce an acceptable level of law and order, and bureaucratic probity.

Of course, we Welsh have now been permitted to have a devolved 'Assembly'. An 'Assembly' consisting of a collection of self-serving career 'Politicians'. Mediocrities who in the vast majority have no qualifications for public office other than their servile subservience to the orders of their Party chiefs, be they Labour, Tory, Plaid or Liberal Democrat.

I have to affirm that I would prefer to be ruled by idealists such as Julian Cayo-Evans, Denis Coslett, John Barnard Jenkins. Men who placed personal honour and love of their country above self-aggrandisement. Attributes and concepts which appear to be totally lacking in our present political rulers.

With a salute to my father and his friends, I finish.

Sian Dalis Cayo-Evans BA, May 2001

Chapter One

O N THE 1ST OF JULY, 1969, beneath louring grey skies a glittering ceremony took place in the Upper Ward of the ancient Castle of Caernarfon. Surrounded by dignitaries, courtiers, choirs and all the gorgeous panoply of antique ritual the eldest son of the Queen of England knelt before his mother, and placing his hands between hers, vowed,

"I, Charles, Prince of Wales, do become your liegeman of life and limb and of earthly worship, and faith and truth I will bear unto you to live and die against all manner of folks… "

With her own hands Queen Elizabeth placed the orb-topped coronet on her son's head, the Golden Rod of Office into his fingers, and clasped the plush velvet and ermine robe around his shoulders. After the Loyal Addresses had been declaimed the Monarch led the newly invested Prince of Wales up onto the arch of Queen Eleanor's Gate overlooking the square of the small North Welsh town, to present him to his people. But the only burst of full-throated spontaneous cheering to greet their prince came from a group of schoolchildren. The remainder of the spectators outside this particular gate seemed strangely subdued.

Despite the crowds thronging the streets of Caernarfon there had not occurred the anticipated influx of foreign tourists for this occasion. Many of the specially built carparks were only partially filled. Some celebrities such as Richard Burton and Elizabeth Taylor had cancelled their visit; and due to an alarming American television report about bombs being planted in the town, screened in the States some days previously, planeloads of American and Canadian people of Welsh stock had also cancelled their reservations.

The absence of so many thousands of expected onlookers was compensated for however by the presence of thousands of gun-carrying Special Branch and CID detectives and uniformed police patrolling the streets, and the further thousands of heavily armed soldiers equipped with all the sophisticated paraphernalia needed for a maximum security operation in the town's environs.

A security operation made necessary by what was happening on that same day far to the South in the grim courtroom of the Glamorgan Assizes at Swansea. There a group of other Welshmen were hearing their jail sentences from the lips of Sir John Thompson, Judge of the High Court... Julian Cayo Evans, Denis Coslett, Keith Griffiths, Antony Lewis, Vivian Davies, Vernon Griffiths; one by one the men were dealt with, and with the judge's measured words the second longest trial in Welsh legal history came to its close. For 53 days the story of what these men, and others like them, had done, had been unfolded before the fascinated attention of the nation.

They were rebels who had attempted the arguably impossible. To raise a resurgent Celtic nation into open conflict against the Government of Westminster and the British Crown. They had tried to challenge and overthrow one of the most stable and entrenched systems of government in the world. Attempting this task without any safe area to organise from, to train in, or to retreat into. Their resources minute, their total numbers of necessity limited; and the very people they hoped to raise in rebellion for the most part uncaring, apathetic, and many actively hostile to their aims.

They had styled themselves the Free Wales Army, and they swore allegiance only to the proud emblem of their forefathers, *Y Ddraig Goch*, the Red Dragon banner of the Cymry.

* * *

Unlike Ireland there was no unbroken tradition of bloody resistance to English rule in Wales. After the failure of Owain Glyndŵr in the early years of the 15th Century to drive the Anglo-Norman conquerors from Welsh soil, it seemed that the two nations of England and Wales were destined to be forever joined in indivisible union; and for hundreds of years Welshmen and Englishmen fought side by side to enlarge the boundaries of the British Empire. Yet there was always a persistent thread of discord and resentment running through the pattern of union. In the mountain areas the Welsh people jealously guarded their ancient language and culture, stubbornly resisting all attempts at Anglicisation. But this was only a rearguard action which could do nothing to prevent the erosion of the language, and the decay of Celtic culture and tradition where industry blighted the once-green valleys and hills. Even the march of the Hosts of Rebecca, and the armed clash at Newport in 1839 between Welshmen and Scottish troops were more an indication of social unrest than nationalistic fervour.

By the dawn of the 20th Century it seemed that the Welsh were nothing more than Western English. The Welsh schoolteachers paid service to this belief by punishing those children who persisted in speaking their native tongue and forcing them to wear around their necks wooden boards with the letters *WN* burned into the grain — *"Welsh Not!"* Yet somehow the language survived, as did the oral and sung poetry, the *penillion*, created and performed by the farmers, shepherds and labourers of the mountains. Because of this survival the consciousness of Welsh nationhood was kept alive, and with the foundation of *Plaid Cymru*, the Welsh Nationalist Party, in 1925 came the hope for those of Nationalist beliefs that an independent Wales could be won through the ballot box. The party remained ineffectual, without any widespread voting support or representation in the London Parliament.

The relationship between England and Wales remained unchanged, and their disputes were fought out on the rugby field rather than the debating chamber. Then in 1936 three leading members of Plaid Cymru used violent methods of protest against what they regarded as an example of English oppression. The Llŷn Peninsula in North Wales, a place of great scenic beauty, was commandeered for use as a bombing school range for the RAF. Many Welsh people bitterly opposed the selection of this site, and Saunders Lewis, D.J. Williams, and Lewis Valentine, respectively university lecturer, school teacher and Baptist minister, set fire to the sheds of the bombing school in protest, then immediately surrendered themselves to the police. They were regarded as heroes by many of the local population and at their trial in Caernarfon despite their pleas of guilty, the local jury could not agree to bring in a verdict. A re-trial was held at the Old Bailey in London and the all-English jury quickly found them guilty. The three were sent to prison in Wormwood Scrubs serving nine months each.

Their isolated gesture was not forgotten by Welsh Nationalists, but it was not until 1952 that violence again intruded into Anglo-Welsh relations. This was an unsuccessful attempt to blow up a pipeline leading from the new Claerwen dam in mid-Wales to Birmingham. The attempt was made by members of a small republican movement, Y Gweriniaethwyr. Again the slight ripple of excitement subsided, and it seemed that any dream of a free Wales controlling its own natural resources had gone from the hearts and minds of the Welsh.

But resentment of English domination still lingered in some quarters, and the smouldering spark of nationalism was ready to burst into flame if the right tinder could be found. That tinder was supplied by the building of yet another dam, whose waters drowned the valley of Tryweryn and the village of Capel Celyn; and the ignited spark of nationalism roared into the blasting flames of exploding bombs.

Chapter Two

THE VALLEY OF TRYWERYN, the valley of the Holly Tree, one of the most beautiful and picturesque valleys in Wales, set high in the mountains of Meirionydd supported a farming community of some seventy people. The community centred itself upon the small grey-rock village of Capel Celyn. The people were quiet and law-abiding, content to work their farms and live their traditionally austere lives which revolved around their homes and chapel. The one-time Postmistress of Capel Celyn, Mrs Harriet Parry had spent all her life in the valley and its environs. To her, her husband Tom and their daughter Bethan, it was their home and they wished for no other…

"It was a very small village, the chapel, my post office and the school for about twenty children; Miss Richards was the Head Teacher. Then there were two houses by the school and seven houses further down, and the farms of course, Gelli, Cae Fadog, Tyrpeg and the others. We had one unique building though. It was a tiny Sunday School, the first ever built in the whole world. That's not much, I know, but it was unique, and it was ours… My husband loved the Celyn, it was such a friendly village. He used to go to shoot on the mountain, and to fish. It was a good fishing place at the bottom of our garden where the river ran.

"Then one day, Bethan, my daughter was only about ten years old and she came from school, and when we were having our tea she said… 'They're going to drown this village, Mam, and the fields, and everything… '"

During the mid-Fifties with what seemed to be a measured arrogance the Liverpool Corporation earmarked the valley for a reservoir, and without consulting Meirionydd County Council began the legal processes necessary to acquire the site. In Capel Celyn a defence committee was formed and 125 local authorities, trades union branches, religious and cultural organisations rallied to its support, collecting petitions and passing resolutions condemning the scheme. Liverpool Corporation reacted indignantly.

"We need this new reservoir for our 600,000 population," their spokesman claimed. "Without it they'll go thirsty!"

This was a blatant deception. More than sufficient domestic water was already being supplied from the Lake Fyrnwy reservoir. This water from Tryweryn was wanted for a proposed industrial expansion, and for profitable re-sale.

Realising the strength of feeling in Wales the majority of the Welsh members of Parliament jumped on the bandwagon of protest and came out against Liverpool. At the second reading of the scheme's promoting Bill in the House of Commons 27 of the 36 Welsh MPs voted against it, and the rest abstained.

The Liverpool Corporation pressed on, refusing even to receive any delegations to discuss the scheme. Gwynfor Evans, leader of Plaid Cymru, journeyed to Liverpool and tried to address the Corporation members in session. He created an uproar and his words were drowned out by the members shouting and banging their desks. Finally he was bodily ejected from the chamber by the police. The people of Capel Celyn in a despairing gesture marched in protest through the streets of Merseyside, and were virtually ignored. Harriet Parry was on that march...

"... It was terrible when they said we'd have to move. Everybody was upset except for one family who thought they were going to get a lot of money. But nobody got all that much money, and money didn't count anyway… Except for that family nobody else was willing to move. We had meetings in the chapel about it, and three busloads of us went to Liverpool to protest. The police were very good to us, they came to meet us at the entrance to that big tunnel, and stayed with us all day.

"We walked up and down the streets, we had banners and everything. The people in the streets didn't pay much attention to us. We walked right up to the Corporation offices, but they wouldn't come out to face us. We sang old Welsh ballads and hymns outside, and my daughter, Bethan, recited a poem. Nothing happened. David Roberts, he had Cae Fadog farm and was a deacon at our chapel, he went into the offices to ask them if they would consider our protest, but they wouldn't. It had all been settled and gone through long before we had started protesting I'm sure… "

Following this march, and perhaps ashamed of their previous ill-manners, the Liverpool Corporation then invited Gwynfor Evans to address them, and this time heard him out in silence. His pleas moved few hearts. A vote was taken upon the matter, and 90 of the 160 councillors voted to drown the village. One Labour councillor who voted against the motion was expelled from his party.

Meanwhile the Lord Mayor of Cardiff had been active, convening a national conference which prepared an alternative reservoir scheme. This would still entail the use of part of the Tryweryn Valley, but would have spared the village and much of the farmland. Because it would have been more expensive to implement, this alternative was brusquely rejected by the Liverpool Corporation, who refused to meet the representatives of the conference.

July 1957 brought the third reading of the Bill in the House of Commons. The promoters and opponents came to an arrangement not to debate the issue and the Bill went through in only minutes, to be given an equally accelerated passage through the House of Lords. The people of Capel Celyn lost heart. It was apparent that despite the bitter opposition of Welsh public opinion, the constitutional processes had failed those very minorities they were supposed to safeguard.

The Minister for Welsh Affairs, Henry Brooke, knew something of Welsh values, but even he, it appeared, would only help the seemingly all-powerful Liverpool Corporation.

"Water shortages might occur in the next few years on Merseyside," he declared. "I cannot believe that preservation of the Welsh way of life requires us to go as far as that... "

Faced with such politicians the Welsh people could have been forgiven for wondering if the preservation of Westminster required their help.

The Welsh *Western Mail* stated: "There has been every appearance of complete contempt for Welsh opinion on the part both of the Liverpool Corporation, and of Parliament!"

Perhaps the writer had been present when a Queen's Counsel representing Liverpool held up a pamphlet written by Gwynfor Evans protesting the decision to drown the valley, and said, "This is the best six-pennyworth I have read. But that hardly matters, since we have the power... "

The power he boasted of having was not exercised with the open brutality that such arrogant statements might lead people to expect. But nevertheless, exercised it was. Harriet Parry and her small family were the last inhabitants to leave the village.

"I felt very bitter about having to move, very bitter, but of course everybody else did. The officials from the Liverpool Corporation kept coming every day to ask us when we were leaving. The main official to come round was a Mr Stilgoe, the Liverpool water engineer. He was always very nice and pleasant, I must say that. He and the others used to tell me always, 'Ohhh this isn't good land here, it's only fit for sheep… ' I used to tell them: 'Well we've always managed to pay our way with it.' They used to tell me, 'You'll have a nice new rented house down in Frongoch.'

" 'Home isn't made from bricks and mortar only!' I used to tell them. 'If we wanted a new house down in Frongoch, we'd buy one!'

"My husband wasn't well in health, and when the officials used to come I had to talk with them. My husband was too angry to talk, he was so upset about leaving. So at last they came one morning and asked me, 'Are you ready to go today, Mrs Parry?' 'No,' I said. 'Not today!' They went away and came back in a little while, and asked me to fetch my husband. They told us both that we'd got to move then and there. They'd brought a removal van and a lorry to shift the furniture. The water was already starting to fill up the village, so I knew that there was nothing more to be done.

"The men with the lorry and van were quite kind, but of course with all the dirt thrown up by the machinery our furniture was made filthy. Anyway, when the van left we looked at our home for the last time and began to walk out from the village. There sounded a great crashing noise, and we stopped to look back. A big JCB machine was smashing our house down. My husband was really upset, very very upset. I can see his poor face in my mind now. It was terrible to see our home treated like that. I still feel how I felt that day, even now. I never look at that lake up there, nor my daughter, Bethan, nor my husband would look at it when they were both alive still… We all hated it. We hated that lake… "

With almost unbelievable obtuseness, the Liverpool Corporation were later to invite the Parry family to the official opening ceremony of the Tryweryn Dam.

*   *   *

There were men in Wales however who were still ready to challenge the power of the Liverpool Corporation and the politicians of Westminster; and they were not content to challenge merely with written pamphlets.

"I was then a member of Plaid Cymru, but for years it seemed that the party was powerless to defend the interests of the Welsh people; it was a continuous series of frustrations. These gradually convinced me that something more was needed than petitions and peaceful demonstrations… Tryweryn brought my feelings to a head. There was a demonstration there, and letters of protest, petitions and meetings, and the Liverpool councillors just laughed at them and walked right in. No notice was ever taken by the authorities of the feelings of ordinary men and women.

"Several of us had made up our minds before the formation of the Free Wales Army, that something had to be done about Tryweryn. Something more dramatic than a few letters to the press, and signatures on a roll of paper. A more direct action would have to be taken. We decided that because we had no explosives we would have to think other methods.

"There were four of us, and we scouted the site. One chap knew something about transformers, and he knew that by draining them off considerable damage could be done. So we decided that while two of us went for the transformer, the other two would attempt to destroy the stores and materials at the other end of the valley.

"I remember it was a Saturday night we set out for Tryweryn in an old car. It was a clear night and on the way up I briefed our driver. I told him where we would turn off the main road into the valley. '… When we turn you must switch off the headlamps and go down quietly,' I told him. The damned fool kept the lights on too long and we were spotted from the works site… I and my companion tried to get to the stores huts, but the security men intercepted us, and we had to head up into the hills to make our escape. On the other side of the valley the other two took advantage of the diversion and were able to reach and drain the transformer. They then made for the road to a pre-arranged pick-up point, but the police cars caught them. They mistook a police car without lights for our own. Dai Pritchard and Dai Walters were their names. They later appeared at Bala magistrates court defended by a solicitor named Elystan Morgan, who despite his later bad relationships with FWA men did a superb job of this defence, and they got away with a fine. This was just individuals acting. It was amateurish, and I knew then that we must do better than this. We must get organised, and do some real damage…"

The real damage was soon to occur. On the 10th of February, 1963 a transformer at the Tryweryn damsite was blown up with a gelignite bomb. One of the men responsible had travelled a long distance to carry out this action. Across the width of the North American continent and the Atlantic Ocean.

Chapter Three

THE WAVES OF RESENTMENT bursting from the hearts of some Welsh people over the destruction of Tryweryn sent out wide-spreading ripples, strong enough to reach as far as Canada, where a black-haired, grey-eyed young Welshman named Owain Williams was working in the tough logging camps of British Columbia. He possessed fervent nationalist convictions, which he had held since boyhood.

"When nationalism started for me, I know it seems ridiculous, I was only nine years old. My mother bought me a book for my birthday about Owain Glyndŵr. What interested me in it from the first was finding out that Wales had been a nation so long ago. This book had a lot of influence on me, possibly because it was one of the few we had in the house written in Welsh, and I couldn't read or speak English then. I learned that language at school when I was about ten or eleven years old.

"My father was the tenant of quite a big farm near Nefyn, about 450 acres, and we were four brothers in the family, so at that time there wasn't any money to spare, or much food either come to that. The owner used to come round once a year collecting the rents and shooting the pheasants, we used to joke that he was shooting the peasants. He was English, or maybe Anglicised Welsh, dead now, rest his soul.

"When he came collecting the rents the old people always followed the traditional ways of acting towards the landlord. My father used to take his cap off when speaking to him, even if it was raining he still took it off and stood there with

Owain Williams

the water running down his neck. This annoyed me when I was a kid, I used to think the world of my father you see. He was the best man living to me. When I used to see the rain running down his face I used to feel like going and kicking the landlord in the shins. I remember one year our old dog, who was half-blind, lifted his leg and pissed over the landlord's plus-fours. I was so pleased I went and cut the dog a big piece of bread and jam, and there was never much jam in the house those days.

"When I was about eleven I joined Plaid Cymru. They didn't know my age, I just sent a form and got a card and badge of membership. I dropped out of the party when I was sixteen because I didn't see much hope in them for a Welsh nation. I thought a lot about emigrating, and later after I was married and my first child, a girl, Eiriona, was three months old, my wife and I crossed over to Canada. It was a good life there, I worked on various ranches in the Fraser Valley near Vancouver, but always I felt drawn back to Wales.

"I began doing spells in the logging camps in British Columbia. The work was hard but the wages were good, and I needed the money because by then my son, Griff, had been born. My mother always sent me the newspapers from Wales, and from 1957 onwards there were frequent reports about the proposed flooding of Tryweryn, and the uproar that it was causing back home. The attitude in Wales about Tryweryn was in my mind constantly. There was a lot of talk and hot air being blown about, but I thought that as usual no one would actually do anything about it. Then in one logging camp I met a couple of French Canadians. They interested me because there weren't many of them on the West Coast. We became good friends and they told me that they were members of the FLQ, the Freedom for Quebec movement. They knew explosives and they showed me a few things about them. I hadn't ever seen a stick of gelignite before, but my friends soon taught me all the basics.

"More letters and newspaper cuttings about Tryweryn were sent to me, and I began to think that if I went back to Wales with my new knowledge about explosives, maybe I could do something about the situation. At least show that the spirit of Wales was still alive. Because I thought it was very arrogant the way the Liverpool Corporation was going about it, you know, pushing this little valley of a hundred people around because it's always so easy for the big to crush the small. So at last, in late 1959, I decided to return to Wales.

"To support my family I bought a little coffeebar cum restaurant in Pwllheli, North Wales, and for a couple of years worked all the hours I could stay awake to build up trade. Also I started preparing to do some action at Tryweryn. A lot of young people and students came to my coffeebar and amongst them there was quite a lot of strong feeling against this flooding. There seemed to be growing a semi-resurgence of nationalism. A lot of them appeared to have the same sort of feelings as myself, but I couldn't be sure that their ideas matched with the courage of convictions necessary to carry out some sort of action. In Wales there are a good many equivalents of Ireland's Guinness Republicans, great talkers in their beer, great talkers even without the beer.

"Then I met Emyr Llewelyn, a curly-headed student at the University of Wales, who was the son of a well known bard. Normally I'm a bit dubious of students. They tend to talk a lot, drink a lot, and mix their talk and their drinks. But this one had special qualities. He was a very quiet and serious guy, and took a long while to decide to give his trust. We had a great many discussions, and slowly we evolved our ideas. We would form a small organisation, a resistance group. We chose the name, *Mudiad Amddiffyn Cymru*, in English, 'Movement for the Defence of Wales'. The initials would form the word MAC, which stuck in peoples minds easily, and was also a back-handed jibe at the establishment politician, Harold Macmillan, the 'Super-Mac' that the media loved. We recruited another guy, an RAF policeman, John Albert Jones into the group, and found two or three others who, while not being allowed into the inner circle of the MAC, could be used for various jobs. A raid on a quarry netted us a couple of thousand detonators and some gelignite, and we were ready to take action.

"My original plan was to destroy the Tryweryn site completely. To blow up the bridge carrying the site traffic, to blow up the oil dumps, trucks, machinery, everything, hit it out! Emyr wanted to commit only a symbolic act. To be honest I wasn't really interested in that, I don't think symbolism gets you anywhere. Emyr's argument was: 'If we do one symbolic act, we'll be patriots. If we do a lot of damage, we'll be terrorists!'

"Now obviously we didn't want to kill anybody. We're not so vicious as to hurt or kill some innocent person who just happens to be working on the dam. So we went to a lot of trouble, and did a lot of dummy runs, to be able to choose a time when the site would be closed. We had to be very careful because some guys had been there before us and drained oil from a generator. I didn't know who they were, but it meant that there was now a lot more security at the place. They had patrols with Alsatian dogs and tripwires etc. So we had to time blowing the transformer between the checks made by the security men.

"Again we took great pains to establish the site's routine because from any point of view it wouldn't be a good thing to hurt innocent people. We only wanted to hit the site itself.

"On the night of the actual operation, February 10th, nearly everything went wrong. The old Ffestiniog/Tryweryn road across the mountains was blocked with snow, so we had to retrace our route and go round by the Dolgellau/Bala road. Halfway to Bala we blew a tyre and went lurching all over the road, with a bomb in the boot of the car! The car had been hired by Emyr and we found that it had no jack, so there was nothing else for it but for John Jones and myself to hold the car up while Emyr frantically shoved stones and bits of wood scraped from out of the snow under the axle to keep it raised while we changed the wheel. Fortunately no police car came along to act as a Good Samaritan while we were straining our spines.

"We drove on through Bala and turned west through Frongoch village towards the site. We parked the car at a farm, Tai'r Felin, a couple of miles away from Tryweryn and went across country. All the way the snow had covered everything so we kept falling waist deep into ditches and cracking our shins on hidden rocks. Finally we came into sight of the floodlights on the dam site, so then to avoid any sighting we had to crawl on our bellies for about half a mile; and by now all of us were completely saturated to the skin.

"The various hold-ups had thrown the prepared schedule right out, so we had to lie in the shadow of the hedge, watching and listening for a couple of hours until we had made sure that the watchmen were keeping to their normal routine. Then Emyr and myself climbed the perimeter fencing while John stayed outside on watch. The bomb was about five pounds of gelignite sellotaped into a biscuit tin, and the clock was a normal Venner time switch. We placed it right under the oil tank of the transformer, set it to explode at two o'clock, and went back towards the car, still crawling and using cover as much as possible.

"Unfortunately our troubles weren't over yet. It was now past ten o'clock and we couldn't risk going back through Bala because the pubs would be turning out and there would be police wandering around. So we headed towards Betws-y-Coed. More bad luck! A short distance along as we rounded a bend at speed, there in front of us was a van jammed into a snowdrift and blocking the road. The van's driver came straight over to us and I assumed my best English accent while talking with him. Eventually with the three of us pushing and shoving we got both vehicles through and away we went.

"The news of the explosion came over on the TV news the next afternoon. I remember a policeman from Bala standing there with his bicycle and trouser clips stating that there had been three men involved judging from the footprints in the snow, and that one of them had been wearing winkle-picker shoes. That was me so I immediately burned the shoes and we thought we were in the clear. Emyr went back to college, and me to the counter and all seemed well.

"A few days later I heard that Emyr had been arrested. The van driver, a butcher's nephew from Ceredigion and strangely enough a nationalist himself, had told one of his uncle's customers about the three Englishmen in a red Vauxhall car who had helped him from the snowdrift. That customer told the police, and the police checked with the hire companies etc. and found that Emyr had rented a red Vauxhall on the day of the explosion. Fortunately for us the butcher's nephew couldn't identify our features because of the dark. He hadn't been wearing gloves though, and the police found his palm-print still intact on the rear of our car. Of course we were so unused to this sort of thing then that it never occurred to any of us to notice if he had worn gloves as we had… "

On the 29th March, 1963, Emyr Llewelyn Jones was convicted of sabotaging the transformer and sentenced to one year's imprisonment. He refused to identify his two companions and they could not be found or prosecuted.

This type of direct action placed the leaders of the official nationalist party, Plaid Cymru, in an uncomfortable dilemma. The failure of their constitutional strategy had been glaringly exposed by the progress of the dam construction at Tryweryn. Yet the party leadership had been unable, or unwilling, to capitalise on the contemptuous disregard shown for Welsh public opinion and MPs by the Liverpool Corporation. David Pritchard and David Walters, the men convicted and fined for draining the oil from the Tryweryn transformer were both executive members of Plaid Cymru. Now here was another member using a bomb to make his protest. In an attempt to retain some authority over his militants, Gwynfor Evans, Plaid Cymru's leader issued a statement expressing his sympathy with Emyr Llewelyn, and he had previously issued a statement concerning the two previous offenders, saying in it that it should be the English authorities in the dock for these offences, and not these young Welshmen driven by circumstances.

Owain Williams, chairman of the Pwllheli youth branch of Plaid Cymru didn't issue a statement, he preferred to make his protest against his friend's sentence in another manner. . .

"The night that Emyr was sent to prison, myself and John Albert Jones went to blow the pylon at Gellilydan as a protest against his sentence. We didn't want to risk cutting power supplies to hospitals or other essential services so instead of the 280,000 volts cable leading out of the Trawsfynydd Power Station, we chose the 170,000 volt cable leading into the station from the hydro-electric scheme. It was a dark night and drizzling heavily, so in order to keep dry we wore oilskins and big Korean-war type overboots. On the way John said,

'They'll be looking for two bloody Yetis judging by the size of the footprints we're leaving in the slush this time.'

"I hadn't been able to get hold of a time switch so I told John that I'd have to touch the wires by hand. He became increasingly nervous as we fixed the charges to each of the four legs of the pylon, and although I didn't blame him for that, his fright was affecting me. In the end he ran off, I nearly followed him, what with the wind and the rain and the thought that with such a limited length of wires the bloody pylon could well come down on me.

"There was a bridge close by and by stretching the contact wires to their full extent I was able to huddle against the buttress, thinking that if the pylon fell across the bridge I'd be sheltered to some degree. Then just as I was about to touch the wires and blow the charges the thought struck me that perhaps the cables would electrocute the ground. The only comfort that I could derive in that case, was that I wouldn't feel a thing. 170,000 volts would crisp me in a single flash. I screwed up what little courage remained to me and touched the wires. Only two of the charges blew. Through lack of experience, and working mostly by touch in the dark, I'd set the charges wrongly. The pylon shook and swayed on its two remaining legs, and for a few moments I was too petrified to move. I had the unreasoning fear that if I did so, my movement would bring the whole lot down on top of me. Now we were only about a mile from the nuclear station at Trawsfynydd, and the next thing I knew there was a hell of a racket as police cars seemed to come from all over the place with sirens screaming, lights flashing, all heading for the station. This got me moving, and we got away down a little track.

"I rang the police next day and told them that the explosion had been done by MAC as a reprisal for Emyr Llewelyn, and warned them that there were still two unexploded charges. Of course the *Western Mail* immediately slammed our action, saying that we had deliberately tried to cut hospital supplies etc. That was ridiculous, but typical of them… "

For a few days following the pylon blast Owain Williams was able to concentrate on his domestic affairs. His wife had recently given birth to their second daughter, but tragically the baby was suffering from hydrocephalia and both she and her mother were taken back into hospital for treatment. Owain, racked by anxiety, could only wait and hope. Then ill fortune struck again.

One of the fringe members of MAC had been storing the box of detonators. He had been told to burn the box and hide its contents, but with stupid carelessness he merely threw the container into some gorse bushes close to his home. Some children building a bonfire found the box and were carrying it to their fire when a farmer working nearby spotted the warning signs printed on the side of it. He told the children to leave it lying and immediately informed the police. With dogs they tracked the scent back to the fringe-member's house. The man panicked; showed the police his cache of detonators buried in the garden, and named Owain Williams and John Albert Jones as the men who had given them to him. The investigating officers wasted no time…

"The police came to my coffeebar on Sunday night as I was closing and doing my till. I had to open seven days a week to survive there. There were a large crowd of them, all in plainclothes and they came through the kitchen. To give myself time to think I turned round and pretending I didn't know who they were, told them.

'I'm sorry, we're closed for the night.'

'That's alright,' one answered.

'The coffee machine is off.'

'We don't want coffee.'

The conversation was getting a bit forced, but I pressed on.

'Is it cigarettes you want?'

'No, we don't want cigarettes.'

'Oh!' Before I could ask them if they wanted fruit pies, a little cocky one with his hat on the back of his head told me. 'It's you we want Williams, and I've got a warrant for your arrest.'

"They took me to the police station which was just around the corner from my place, and over the next ten hours kept questioning me, while I denied everything. They'd been very busy. They'd raided John Albert's house and had found the overboots we'd worn on the night of the explosion. They'd also taken a plaster-cast of our car tyre from a molehill I'd run over at the pylon site. I'd been using my father's car that night, and of course the cast fitted. There were a few other things as well, such as people telling them about Emyr Llewelyn stopping at my café etc. I must admit we were very much amateurs about security at that time, but I couldn't help admiring the police forensic methods and their expertise.

"I was worried about my elder kids being alone in the flat above the café, and I told the police this. After some time they took me upstairs and to a window facing the back of my place. Then they asked me to sign statements about the transformer at Tryweryn, pinching the explosives from the quarry, and of course the pylon. I wouldn't do this. But some time later the light in my flat's bedroom went on and I could see the police in the room. They held my kids up against the window so that I could see them; and they were both crying and frightened. This is bloody true, the bastards did this. I signed every statement, I wanted my kids to be left alone, not frightened half to death… It's amazing how scared the authorities are of anything that smacks of a political motive. Every day people kick children downstairs, break their bones, torture and kill them, and get patted on the head by do-gooders and walk out of court on probation. But if anything looks tinged with political motivation, the authorities react frantically and come down hard.

"Having said that, I must also say that the judge I went in front of was fairly lenient, giving me a year on each of the three charges. There was actually a lot of pressure in our support, an amazing amount, both from Welsh political circles and from private people. Of course the police went into my background to try and find anything to blacken my character with. But there was nothing. I'd never pinched a dime in my life, always tried to live honestly in fact.

"Prison wasn't too hard. The worst thing was that my little baby had to have a brain operation while I was inside. It was a hell of a worry. The governor actually let me out for one day to go and see her. By myself as well. I respected him greatly for that. Some of the screws jumped on me a bit because I was a political prisoner, but on the whole they were pretty good. I remember one of the bad ones especially though. A Welshman from Cydweli, an old Principal Officer. He was very anti-political. In fact he was anti-coloured, anti-Irish, anti-everything but himself. One day an Irishman came in, the poor devil couldn't read or write.

'Thick bastard!' the Principal Officer said disgustedly. 'All the Irish are thick bastards! Can't do anything! Can't read! Can't write their names! Only shag shag shag and breed bloody kids! It was the same when I was in India, fucking Indians! All they could do was shag all day… I used to shag this young Indian girl! Used to shag dozens of them, bloody animals they are!'

"This is all the man ever talked about, all day, every day, it used to get on my nerves. Sometimes he'd dig at me, saying,

'Wouldn't you be better off with your wife tonight? I wonder who she's with?' I hated him for it at the time, but unhappily it did break my marriage up in the end, being in prison. I'm sure the women here bitterly resent their husband being involved with a cause. Yet in Ireland it's totally different. The women there are very loyal to their menfolk. Usually the women also come from families who are very Republican, there's a long tradition of that in Ireland, but not in Wales.

"I think the most lasting memory of prison comes from when I was working in the kitchens at Drakes Hall open nick. One day, this was in 1963, a little fellow from Pontypŵl went to the fridge and pulled out a leg of lamb stamped *New Zealand 1947*. He shouted… 'Hey Taff, look at this leg of lamb. It's no lamb at all, its a bloody teenager!"

Chapter Four

WITH THE IMPRISONMENT of its three organisers, the first MAC organisation became moribund. But their actions had struck a chord in the emotions of other nationalists, and as Owain Williams had hoped, it showed that the spirit of Wales was still alive. *Cymdeithas yr Iaith Gymraeg*, the Welsh Language Society, made its first major appearance in the political life of Wales by holding a mass demonstration in February 1963 at Aberystwyth, urging equal status for both the English and the Welsh languages in the Principality. A little later there was a sit-down on the Trefechan bridge at Aberystwyth when the police declined to arrest sixty demonstrators plastering inflammatory posters on the town's public buildings.

The protesters held up traffic for an hour and clashed with frustrated motorists and bus-drivers. Local youths, hungry for excitement and seeing the police conspicuously absent, used their fists freely on the men and women activists. The story was splashed all over the dailies the following Monday and in the ensuing uproar, Gwynfor Evans once again came forward, this time to congratulate the Language Society on its actions.

All over Wales painted slogans spread like a rash on walls, bridges, hoardings and rocks... "COFIA DRYWERYN," ("REMEMBER TRYWERYN") "ENGLISH GO HOME!" "ENGLISH OUT!" "STOP STEALING WELSH RESOURCES!" "RESIST ENGLISH RULE!"

Then another completely new slogan appeared which

eventually would outnumber the rest... "FREE WALES ARMY! F.W.A." With it was the large heraldic-shorthand emblem of a white eagle. It was the visible symbol of the ancient legend of the 'White Eagles of Snowdon', who from their lofty crags would rise to repel any invaders who threatened to destroy Wales. Beneath the emblem was written in Welsh... "FE GODWN NI ETO!" ("We shall rise again!")

It was to be a prophetic warning...

Chapter Five

THURSDAY, OCTOBER 21st 1965. The great dam at Tryweryn was ready to be opened and a long convoy of cars and coaches carrying some four hundred official guests passed through Bala heading for the damsite. At the tiny village of Frongoch, once the site of an internment camp for Irish rebels, a young Welshman sitting astride a powerful motorbike sighted the oncoming vehicles and roared off ahead of them up to the dam. There, massed upon the road atop of the dam wall hundreds of men, women and children waving Welsh flags and sloganned banners saw the motorcyclist and knew that the time for their protest had come.

In the leading cars Alderman David Cowley, Lord Mayor of Liverpool, and Alderman Frank Cain, Chairman of the Liverpool Water Committee, unaware of what awaited them, admired the magnificent view of sun-glinted Arenig Fach, the ponderous mountain bordering the western edges of their city's man-created lake. Beneath the centre of the curving dam wall were the modern ugly block of the control building; and close to them a refreshment marquee, a covered platform and a grandstand had been erected for the shelter and sustenance of the speechmaking VIPs and their audience.

As the lead cars swung onto the road that topped the dam the waiting demonstrators surged in front and around them, some men and girls throwing themselves down before the wheels, while others hammered the cars' bodies and

The "welcome in the hillsides" for Liverpool's Lord Mayor and Corporation

roofs with their fists and jeered threateningly. Nearly a hundred uniformed police and CID officers struggled to keep order, and a clear-thinking senior officer managed to extricate the cars from the human sea and divert them back down the hill to the bottom entrance of the dam, where the five coachloads of official guests were debussing near to the control buildings.

The Plaid Cymru officials who had organised the demonstration appealed frantically for order, but at this point a new focus of direction emerged. Three young men carrying Welsh Dragon banners, and wearing peaked green forage caps with White Eagles of Snowdon insignia, suddenly erupted in front of the excited mob. The central figure of the trio, a tall darkly handsome figure, his archaic black riding coat flapping wide about his hips, pointed his banner at the coaches below and shouting for the others to follow, led a howling charge down the sloping banks of the dam.

A solid phalanx of policemen ringed the platform and the yelling, whooping demonstrators surged into them. Stones flew and fireworks exploded as Alderman Frank Cain attempted to make his speech from the platform. His voice abruptly lost its resonant audibility when someone cut the microphone lead. The Lord Mayor, Alderman David Cowley doggedly tried to speak in his turn, but was forced to duck and avoid hurled stones. A tattered Union Jack was set alight and thrown flaming over the high stone parapet of the reservoir outlet, and to a ringing rhythm of blows on the tubular scaffolding of the grandstand the Welsh national anthem thundered from hundreds of impassioned throats.

By now the police had managed to isolate and overpower the three green-capped ringleaders, but this only served to drive the mob into greater excess. An old white-haired hill farmer threw punches at policemen's heads, and all along the heaving line in front of the platform scuffles broke out, kicks and blows thudded into bodies, and men and women grappled, shouted and cursed in fury. The refreshment marquee billowed out and collapsed as its guyropes were slashed, and the specially erected toilets burst into flames. The speechmaking was abandoned in despair and the actual opening of the reservoir was signalled only by the roaring jetting of the water from the turned-on outlet pipes.

Shaken and embarrassed by the unexpected vehemence of the protest the VIPs allowed themselves to be led away, leaving the demonstrators jubilantly celebrating their successful disruption of the ceremony. Yet, to the calmer heads among them it was obvious that they were only celebrating defeat. For the drowned valley was fulfilling the purpose allotted to it by the bureaucrats, and the water was rushing through the pipes towards the taps of Merseyside.

The Lord Mayor, smarting under the gibe that Liverpool people didn't need the water because they washed themselves in Guinness Stout, snarled:

"If I'd brought the Kop with me today there wouldn't have been a murmur out of this lot. They'd have been too afraid to open their mouths. The Kop would eat them!"

Some of the reporters present were intrigued by the military-style caps of the three men held by the police, and were quick to seek interviews with the leader, the tall dark-haired young man, whose name was Julian Cayo Evans. The reporters were even more intrigued when he calmly informed them that he was a Commandant of the Free Wales Army, which until now had been thought to be a myth. A matter solely of painted slogans on bridges and walls. Now, instead of nebulous rumours here was actual open manifestation of an organisation which during the next few years was to attract the attention of the world's media, and to bring swarming into Wales thousands of police, soldiers and Special Branch men of Great Britain's security forces.

*   *   *

Julian William Edward Cayo Evans, known simply as Cayo, was in many senses the most romantically idealistic of the personalities that were to emerge as leaders of the FWA in the coming years. He was a throw-back to the warrior Celts of antiquity, obsessed and enamoured by the horse, the wild mountain country of his native land, and the histories of its ancient Princedoms. His paternal grandfather had been a great horseman, breeding and supplying cavalry mounts to many of the continental armies, and droving cattle into England from his 400 acre farm high in the mountains of Carmarthenshire. Cayo inherited his grandfather's love of horses; his own father, John Cayo Evans, was a brilliant academic who took a Triple First at Oxford and spent 22 years in the Indian Civil Service as Director of Education to the Central Provinces.

When Cayo was born, John Cayo Evans was then 58 years of age, a very tall, balding, grey-moustachioed man whose clothing forever held the scent of the strong tobacco he favoured. At this time, 1938, he was the owner of Glandennis House near the quiet market town of Llanbedr-Pont-Steffan, a turreted Gothic mansion, parts of which had been a monastic Grange farm. He divided his time between his professional post as Professor of Mathematics at the University College of Wales in Llanbedr-Pont-Steffan, and his duties as the Lord High Sheriff of Cardiganshire. Although one of the earliest members of Plaid Cymru, he was still very much a member of the Establishment of the day, a product of Victorian Imperialism. A somewhat dour and stern figure, he treated his son with great kindness, but as the boy grew older realising that he would never be an academic like himself, he seemed to lose interest in him, and the young Cayo was forced to turn more to his mother, becoming very close to her.

The boy's scholastic career was spent in a series of expensive preparatory and boarding schools, lastly the exclusive Millfield Public School in Somerset. Millfield at that period was very much a training ground for the sons of gentlemen, and happily for Cayo, maintained large stables. Although undistinguished academically the boy excelled in horsemanship. Not even a fractured skull sustained when thrown by a horse just after his eleventh birthday could abate his enthusiasm for riding.

It was at Millfield when he was 15 years old that Cayo Evans came into close contact with a man who was to make a deep and lasting impression upon him, and to quicken the growth of the nationalist convictions already taking root in his mind. A languages master, a Polish exile named Yanick Helczman became the boy's housemaster. One day during some free time Cayo was walking past a shoe factory in the town where striking pickets were handing out Communist leaflets. He took the leaflets back to school to read, and Helczman saw him doing so. He took his pupil aside and talked long and seriously to him about the dangers of Communism.

The Pole was a very romantic figure in the school, an army veteran who had fought against both Russians and Germans. He bore scars on his face left by a Cossack sabre, and had taken part in the doomed charges of the Polish cavalry against the Nazi panzers. A fervent nationalist and rabidly anti-communist he greatly influenced the impressionable teenager by his faith in his country, and in his church. Although Cayo did not blindly hero-worship the man, yet he realised that this was a person far removed from the ordinary run-of-the-mill human being. Perhaps the youth, distant in temperament from his own father, was unduly influenced by the ideas and beliefs of the glamorous Pole, yet he found as he grew older that those beliefs and ideals stood the test of time, for himself at least.

After finishing his education Cayo Evans was almost immediately called up for National Service. He went with the army to Malaya, and the messy, gruelling anti-guerrilla operations he was to take part in over the next few years were to help metamorphise his youthful nationalist beliefs into a passionate, bitter conviction of their rightness…

"I served for two years in Malaya as a leading scout of 8 platoon, C company, 1st Battalion, the South Wales Borderers, remaining an ordinary private for my entire service. Later I was to serve in the Territorial Army as an Ensign in the Pembroke Yeomanry, an Ensign being a sort of probationary Lieutenant, that is when one come up from the ranks.

"I couldn't claim to be a brilliant soldier; discipline irked me, but I found the jungle operations very interesting. You could safely call me middle-of-the-road cannon fodder. Anyway, when I finished my service I was given my tin medal for services rendered, which looked quite impressive to the TA recruits. An old county regiment such as ours was run with the utmost rigidity and conscript life meant poor pay, poor food and not much sleep, but it had its compensations. I made some good friends and had a lot of fun at times. Particularly when we got leave to Singapore, where the first step was into a bar, and the next into a brothel where we could indulge our exotic Oriental fantasies for a modest fee.

"We were part of the 17th Ghurka Division which was spread all over the Malay peninsula in garrisons and camps. Most of the operations were with helicopter transport. Out we'd go to a 'dropping zone', to cover the rest of the lads coming in. A few blasts of artillery to give it atmosphere, and off we'd be.

"We used to split up into platoons and sections, each taking a different area as a base, making a camp from which patrols would go out on various missions. Progress is pretty slow in secondary jungle and swamp, sometimes it's only possible to cover a couple or three miles in a day. The monsoons were bloody awful, all our kit constantly soaked through and rotting. Despite the gory epics written about the 'War of the Running Dogs', we seldom ran into the enemy. The Chinese communist platoons were too cunning, and were not hide-bound by rigid rule books of war.

"There was the occasional ambush, and sometimes a grisly humorous incident such as when a sprightly young subaltern put us in an ambush position, then later sneaked back to catch us asleep, and got himself shot twice by one of the lads who was more wide-awake then himself. On another occasion four of us were detailed to carry the corpse of a Chinese guerrilla into the company stores. As we put the deceased down in the gloom he let rip a rattling fart, and four men broke the sprint record for the Far East.

"Towards the end of my service one fact had become indelibly imprinted on my mind. That being how easy it was for small numbers of determined insurgents to tie up many thousands of regular troops, and almost paralyse the normal governing and administration of vast areas of country. Something else had occurred which was later to change the structure of my life, and indirectly to help lead to my involvement with the Free Wales Army. In the British army I first met Irish Republican sympathisers, and I listened to the stories they told of the struggle for Irish freedom, and the fight against the Black and Tans in which some of their older relatives and friends had played their parts. I was later to read every book I could find on the subject, and also to delve deeply into Irish history, music and folklore, not knowing then that one day I would be honoured by the people of Ireland for my own part in the struggle for the dignity and freedom of our own Welsh nation.

"I completed my National Service and spent a year at the Agricultural College in Cirencester, then returned to Wales and began breeding Appaloosa and Palomino horses, and won three British championships with a stallion. Like many other Welshmen I read about the destruction of Capel Celyn, and felt a deep anger at the arrogance of the political hacks responsible for it. When I first saw the signs depicting the 'White Eagles of Snowdon' on walls etc. it came as a personal thrill. I thought that at last Welshmen were protesting, and perhaps preparing to stand up and do something about the total disrespect of our rights and sovereignty shown by England towards us Welsh. Instead of the whining, licking-one's-wounds-in-the-corner patriotism of Plaid Cymru, there now seemed to be emerging a militant resurgence of the Welsh soul.

"With my nationalist background and beliefs, and my fairly specialised military training and experience, after seeing the slogans and the White Eagles, I began to wonder how I could get in touch with the FWA, and offer my services as a volunteer. I realised that for the last five hundred years 90% of the Welsh people had grovelled to their English rulers and adapted to the feudal mores of England: reward to the informer, gibbet for the patriot, and sinecures and pensions for those within the castle walls. It was the remaining 10% of the Welsh that I identified with, those that had clung to the ashes of our nationhood. I mentally rummaged among those ashes to see what had survived. At one time Wales had fought, gained and held her independence under Owain Glyndwr — his parliament building still stood in Machynlleth. We possessed the most unique and beautiful national flag in the world, the Red Dragon, coupled with the most rousing and stirring of national anthems. Our own breeds of horses and ponies. Our own cattle, the Welsh Blacks, whose origins dated back to the, 9th Iberian Legion of the Roman occupation, fine sheep and pigs. Traditional cuisine and costume. Our language, one of the oldest in the world was still surviving despite erosion and the systematic policy of destruction followed by many English governments. We had vast resources of coal, steel and water, even gold mines and lead mines. Our assets would be the envy of many of the world's independent nations, and yet where was our nation? Did it exist, apart from the fervent rugby crowds on international match days?

"I had never been interested in the culture-vulture nationalist playing dirges on a lofty harp in a draughty pavilion with his patriotism safely submerged in history, and his day to day life spent in the ivory towers of some educational establishment. Equally I disliked the left-wing politics of the trade union officials, replete with plastic macs and duodenal ulcers. Cloth cap and peppermint-sucking politicians would never restore freedom to Wales. What was needed was to combine the latent power of the really die-hard nationalists into a single force, dedicated to gaining independence for our country. But before they could be combined it was necessary to seek them out as individuals.

"I had read the newspaper reports of Owain Williams' trial, and knew that during the proceedings the police had produced documents which they claimed had been found in Owain's possession and were to do with the FWA. So I decided to go to the North and see him after his release from prison in 1964, hoping he would be my entryway into the ranks of this secret army.

"Owain owned this café place, and I went there with a friend, Lyn Ebenezer. He and Owain were known to each other, and Lyn had told him previously how anxious I was to meet the man who seemed to be the focal point of resistance to English mis-government, having bombed Tryweryn and spent time in jail for this.

"The police were keeping Owain under a degree of surveillance so he arranged to meet us after dark at a bridge nearby. We drew up in the car and he joined us from the shadows. We went out to a deserted beach from where we could see the lights of Pwllheli town, and sat on the stones there talking for several hours. I found myself becoming increasingly impressed with this man, he was my kind of nationalist. I asked him point-blank if the Free Wales Army existed, or whether it was merely a wishful dream?

'Yes, indeed it does exist!' he told me, and said that there were several groups of cadres in the North, but as yet none in Middle and West Wales. He himself was not a member due to constant police surveillance, but was sympathetic to their aims.

"Both Lyn and I volunteered our services, but Owain said that from what he knew of the existing cadres they didn't wish for volunteers foreign to their own districts. He suggested that since I had military experience, and knew my home district well, I should form my own group, or Column as we later styled our units, in the area of mid and west Wales. By doing this I should be of much greater service to the cause of Welsh independence. The suggestion appealed strongly to me. I had always been resentful of discipline, but if I organised my own column, then I shouldn't be taking orders, but issuing them.

"Remember that these were very early days for the Free Wales Army. We had not yet formulated any strategic or tactical aims. Our only instinct at that time was to try and do something to fight back against the criminal exploitation of Welsh resources by what we extreme nationalists regarded as an oppressive foreign regime. Being a Welsh speaker who moved in nationalist circles I had met a great many people who professed sympathy with the idea of a resistance movement to English rule. My first impulse was to rush up to them excitedly issuing invitations to all and sundry to come and enlist in my column and join the revolution.

"Fortunately I was able to control my wilder urges. Instead I devoted the next few months to thinking out exactly what I wished to do, and tried to envisage the best ways to organise a column. Of course, like all the rest of my future fellow leaders of the FWA, I still had to make my living, and after I married, to support my young family. For me, a horse-breeder and trainer, that entailed a great deal of hard physical work and a lot of travelling. Unlike the forces that were later deployed against us, we had no unlimited state funds to draw upon. We financed ourselves, and had to earn that finance by our own sweat and toil.

"I decided finally to attempt to form a double-tiered structure. An active force of men, backed up by a hidden force of sympathisers. Later, when the army expanded and many more columns were formed all over Wales, and indeed even in parts of England, my initial simplistic structure was to become a much more involved and sophisticated organisation. Knowing as I did my own inexperience, I could only hope to learn from my mistakes, and formulate my plans as best I could.

"The *Angel* public house in Aberystwyth was a very popular haunt of militant nationalists, so was the *Stag and Pheasant* at Pontarsais near Carmarthen and other pubs such as the *Gors Goch* and *Talgarreg*. At times scores of young and old nationalists would gather in these pubs, singing patriotic songs, playing music and generally enjoying themselves by asserting their fervent patriotism. I started to frequent these gatherings, getting myself known, and also searching for

The early days of the FWA: Cayo Evans and some of his men demonstrating at Aberystwyth

suitable people to join my column. There seemed to be a great number of potential recruits around, mostly disillusioned Plaid Cymru members.

"Looking back I believe that the politicians of Westminster created the Free Wales Army. Men like myself were only the ignition switches needed to set the whole thing in motion. For years the politicians of all parties, Left, Right and Centre had relentlessly exploited Wales for their own self-aggrandisement, and secure in their sinecured arrogance had contemptuously disregarded Welsh public opinion and protest. Their corrupt and dishonest mismanagement, under the pretext of it all being 'good for Britain', had created a tremendous amount of disgusted resentment. The FWA and the other extremist groups were the backlash of that resentment.

"Gradually I recruited the nucleus of what was to become the West Wales Column, and equally gradually built up over my very large area, a small network of sympathisers. People who could be relied upon to act as couriers, provide hiding places, act as drivers etc. I also began my first propaganda exercise by plastering the slogans and emblem of the FWA all across mid and West Wales creating, I hoped, the impression in people's minds that there was a wide-spread secret army already in existence, instead of the comparative handful that we actually were. To give my small group a rest from the paintbrush I took them to demonstrations organised by the Welsh Language Society and others, such as the one at Aberystwyth when Harold Wilson visited the town in his capacity as Prime Minister.

"Inevitably we became frustrated and impatient with what we were doing. Painting slogans and shouting at demonstrations were not really achieving anything to free our country, and although we attracted some degree of interest in our own area we needed to create a much wider platform of support. In this present age the only way to attract widespread attention is through the media, newspapers, television and radio. I began to cast about for some means of utilising the media to achieve the publicity that I considered we needed. The opening of the Tryweryn dam presented me with an opportunity to get that publicity.

"With two of my column, Wyn Jones and Dafydd Williams, I went up there for the opening ceremony. We had bought three peaked army forage caps from a market stall, and had dyed them green and fastened White Eagle badges on a red flash above the peaks: our first attempt at creating a uniform. Each carrying a Welsh Dragon banner we walked towards the crowds gathered on the top of the dam. I felt a lot of trepidation, because we couldn't know how we would be received by the demonstrators. Would they insult us? Or rebuff us? Or jeer and laugh at our crude caps and banners?

"They did none of these things. Instead they turned and looked at us in silence. Then I heard a ripple of comments run through the mass of people. Mostly, 'The Free Wales Army are here!' Suddenly a couple of men cheered and an old fellow came forward and hugged me in welcome, and then the whole crowd started cheering and applauding us, shaking our hands and slapping our shoulders. I kept remembering a line from a poem by Chesterton, 'I too have had my moment of glory.' It was for me a very moving moment, and brought a lump to my throat.

"Overall it was an amazing eye-opener for me. The effect our arrival had was to galvanize a crowd which up to then had been uncertain whether to fight, or to merely stand and watch. When we went down the slope at the police they were only too eager to follow. It left me with the conviction that the Free Wales Army must from now on come out into the open at all times, and be seen to be leading the fight for a free nation. We must try and present a rebel image that the young and old could identify with. Give people something to distract them from the everyday ordinariness of work and television viewing. If you like, we must try to romanticize rebellion… "

* * *

The publicity Cayo Evans had hoped for materialised very quickly; reporters and photographers ever hungry for newsworthy stories made the trek to the Gothic mansion near Llanbedr-Pont-Steffan. The FWA commandant was quick to seize the opportunity to feed the media's appetite.

Some journalists such as Dan O'Neil, were dismissive. Stating that the "… White Eagles were fledglings at the art of sabotage," and that they "… showed little of the fight they had boasted of."

An editorial in the *Western Mail*, one of the most widely circulated papers in the Principality sounded a more alarmist note: "An even more alarming development in the row over Tryweryn has been the emergence into the open of forage-capped 'Free Wales Army' volunteers. If these young buffoons officially disowned by Plaid Cymru are allowed to develop their theme of resistance to English 'domination', Wales could find itself with a miniature IRA in the hands of a lunatic fringe!" The editorial further declared… "Common-sense and Free Wales nationalism do not walk hand in hand, and before we have a shooting war that is completely against the tide of Welsh opinion these young idiots should be held up to the public contempt they deserve." It finished by wondering why the police at Tryweryn did not act against the FWA for wearing uniforms for political purposes, and demanded: "Does not British Law apply to North Wales?"

The *Daily Mail's* Peta Deschamps brought photographer John Smart with her and obtained pictures of Cayo and some of his group wearing semi-military garb, and aiming shotguns from behind ambush positions of fallen trees with the Red Dragon flag waving above them. She wrote a brief article, implying in part of its headlines that it contained "Secrets of a Secret Society… The White Eagle of Snowdon."

John Summers personalised his report under the headline of "Welsh Dragon breathing Fire". He wrote of: "… bullets tearing turf at my feet, ricocheting… I was on manoeuvres with the Free Wales Army… " and made great capital out of Celtic volubility and fervour.

But no matter what the tone of the reports, for the first time the Free Wales Army had been widely splashed in the national press, and Cayo Evans had gained experience and confidence for the future creation and handling of publicity. The appearance at Tryweryn had also brought him other dividends. He had met the leader of a uniformed nationalist group based in South Wales with many contacts in the valleys. A close liaison between the two was to be established, which in turn accelerated the process of forming a confederated nationwide militant independence movement.

Chapter Six

TONY LEWIS HAD ATTEMPTED to bring his own uniformed group of nationalists up to Tryweryn dam, but the motor coach his colleague Keith Griffiths had arranged for transport failed to turn up. Some of the party had eventually managed to hitch a lift with an excursion bus, but by the time they reached Bala, the riot was over.

Lewis, a tall fair-haired Welshman was then about thirty years of age, slightly older than the majority of the active militants. He had become a convert to nationalism during his military service…

"I became a nationalist sympathiser when I was in the air force. That turned me on, when I met with a Frieslander in Germany and he made me see that Wales was also a country. Previously to that I'd never had any nationalist inclinations, my parents and the rest of my family had no nationalist feelings at all. Not surprising really, because anything we ever learnt historically in school was English biased and Norman biased, and if the Welsh were ever mentioned at all it was as rebels, or chieftans from the hills derogated as robbers and thieves. I can't say that I ever met up with any English bias or hostility against me as a Welshman. But in the air force people calling me Taffy all the time made me begin to realise that to them I was a foreigner.

"When I came out of the air force I used to pass by the Plaid Cymru office in Cardiff, and one day I went in and got some pamphlets from them… That's really how all this started. After reading the Plaid Cymru material and talking with its members I became more and more interested.

"Tryweryn really got people thinking. All those Welsh members of Parliament voting against it, yet Liverpool Corporation were able to ride over them, to ride over the political might of the Welsh nation really. One city corporation, over-ruling everybody and so shattering a community. When Emyr Llewelyn blew up the transformer I thought it was good, great! A song was immediately written about it, and of course these actions inspire others to try the same thing.

"In 1964 I was at the Plaid conference in Caernarfon, I went there thinking that perhaps the party should now start acting more militantly. I met others at the conference, including two Scottish activist observers, who were of a similar mind to myself. We went over to see the Tryweryn site, I remember that that Bank Holiday was the day they'd finally closed the road through the deserted village of Capel Celyn. They'd built this lovely new road all round the site, all concrete and tarmac festooned with diversion signs. There were hundreds of sight-seeing tourists come to look at the rape of a community, so we swapped all the signs over and sent the sight-seers down into the muck and mud of Capel Celyn to let them have a closer view of homes wrecked and people's lives uprooted. There was a hell of a performance, cars stuck all over the place... I then decided, from that point, that I'd do all I could to harass the destroyers of Wales.

"In my hometown at Cwmbran I saw the slogans of the FWA painted on the walls, and thought, 'Well it's all happening, let's get on with it.' With Gethin (Keith Griffiths went under his Welsh name of Gethin ap Iestyn) and a few other Plaid Cymru members we formed our own little unit and called ourselves Free Wales Army. I designed a uniform, black trousers and side-cap, khaki shirts with white badges on a black background; these badges were later changed. At this time we were not thinking of military confrontation.

We used the uniforms because they would be far more effective than Plaid Cymru pamphlets in attracting people's attention. A uniform anyway has a catalytic effect on people. If you wear uniforms, you stick together.

"On the day of the Tryweryn demonstration there were hundreds of demonstrators wandering around Bala, and a lot of varied little groups, some quite elderly, in semi-uniform. All these groups were then mingling, most of them were from the North. Julian (Cayo Evans) was pointed out to me, and I introduced myself. That was our first meeting. The national emotion had been dormant for years, but as in all the other Celtic countries the English managed to trigger it off… "

Tryweryn had been the trigger, but right on the heels of that there came the Clywedog bombing!

Chapter Seven

WALES TODAY

Due to the recent bomb successes various MPs have started an outcry against the Direct Action nationalists who advocate violence.

Plaid Cymru is a passive Political Party that follows the Constitutional way of stopping the drowning of Welsh Valleys and Communities. They have asked the London Government and the Birmingham and Liverpool authorities not to go ahead with schemes to drown Welsh Valleys. They have collected signatures for petitions, 'Pleaded' and 'Begged'. The authorities have proved therefore that Constitutional Methods are of no use.

When a Trade Union on behalf of its people negotiates for better conditions, and exhausts all peaceful means to achieve this, does it give up, No! It is forced to use the only alternative, to become militant and STRIKE.

This is what is happening in our country today, negotiations and peaceful means have failed. The alternative and the only one, to become militant and strike.

To strike where and when we can at pipelines, Government Buildings and Government Installations. Until the London Government and the English authorities realise that it is they who are extreme.

They are extremely wrong in thinking that we in Wales can be pushed back further and further.

For now we have our backs to the wall and we begin to speak the only language that they understand "VIOLENCE".

FREE WALES ARMY

In the old county of Montgomeryshire about halfway between the English border and the Welsh coastline is the jaggedly winding, narrow valley of Clywedog. Apparently uncaring of the furore then taking place concerning the flooding of Tryweryn a consortium of 13 English local authorities decided to take over the Clywedog Valley and turn it into a reservoir. There were only six farms in the valley and initially it appeared that the scheme would go unchallenged, but Plaid Cymru officials took note of what was happening, and decided to try and block the takeover by constitutional means.

There was a law extant which said that every person owning any section of land desired by a Corporation etc. must be allowed to get up and state his case for or against the takeover in a public enquiry, no matter where he lived. Thinking to utilise this law Plaid Cymru raised funds from its members by subscription, bought land in the centre of the proposed site, and for a nominal sum sold homesized plots to some 300 sympathisers. These people were scattered all over the world, America, Canada, Germany etc. The Plaid hoped that rather than go to the immense time, trouble and expense required to bring all these widely dispersed landowners together for a public enquiry, the consortium would re-consider their plan to flood the valley. But this was not to be. As one disgusted Plaid Cymru purchaser stated:

"The Powers that Be took one look at the list of landowners and immediately got another law passed, stating that there was no longer any need to call witnesses and interested parties to an enquiry… Then took the land without any further reference to the owners. It was a complete farce! We were never even officially notified of what had occurred. Here was Plaid Cymru using constitutional methods and being contemptuously outflanked. The Plaid attempted to use the machine of law to aid it, and the machine simply adjusted its gears and went in another direction."

The bulldozers, diggers and trucks moved in and soon the curved walls of the dam were rising. An overhead cableway suspended from two 80ft high steel towers was rigged over the dam walls. The cable cars filled with rubble and concrete for pouring rolled backwards and forwards along the thick wire ropes, and the dam rose up and up.

Then one moonlit night in March 1966 four young men came moving cautiously down the slopes of the 1,580ft Fan Hill, which bordered the dam to the North-east. One man went ahead acting as point scout, the others followed some distance behind carrying spools of telegraph wire, detonators and a bundle of Ajax Polar Ammon gelignite sticks. While the scout kept a lookout for the site watchman, his three comrades planted the charges on the nearest of the cable towers. Once finished the four then made their way back up the slopes, the spool-carriers letting the wire trail out behind them. At a spot where they had left a car battery hidden, the scout went on ahead to a previously noted telephone box. Once there he dialled the site office number, and waited. The man on the slopes, holding the ends of the wires above the battery leads watched for the light in the site office to be switched on, knowing that that would mean the watchman was answering the phone and would be far enough away from the explosion's vicinity to come to harm.

The light came on, the wires crackled on the battery leads and the base of the cable tower exploded in flame and hurtling rubble. The tower swayed and crashed down, bringing with it all the intricate network of cableways across the dam wall. Damage estimated initially at from £45,000 to £30,000 had been caused, and the work on the site would be delayed for months.

The men had almost reached their getaway vehicle when one of them dropped a forage cap which he had pushed into his pocket while setting the charges. With the roar of the explosion still echoing from the surrounding hills the men knew that no time could be lost in moving away to safety, because the police would soon be swarming around the site.

It had been three years all but a month since the last bombing attack, and the police reacted strongly. Regional Crime Squad detectives and uniformed officers were drafted into the area and began an extensive search for the bombers. When the lost forage cap was found suspicion centred on the Free Wales Army. But even on the night of the explosion police raids were carried out on the homes of known extremists.

Owain Williams was in bed when Detective Inspector Shaw called. He answered the door wearing his pyjamas and without being allowed to change was frogmarched around the corner to the police station for questioning. When he asked what was the matter the Inspector told him.

"Some other bloody thing's been blown up!"
Williams was delighted with the news. "Good! Let's celebrate! What are you having, Brandy? Whisky?"

"You bloody clown!" the policeman growled disgruntedly.

Cayo Evans was also at his home when five policemen visited him with a search warrant. He told them that he knew nothing about the explosion, that at the last council of war of the FWA held on St. David's day, only four days previous to the incident, there was no mention of any projected operation. None-the-less the police took away his uniform and a lock of his hair for forensic tests. They also took away an old Welsh Republican flag dating from the 1950's; and to leave nothing to chance took a sample of his white Alsatian dog's hair.

The investigations met with failure, and the search was widened. Many young nationalists were pulled in for questioning in all parts of the country, plus one 84 years old woman who was known to have attended a meeting some eight miles from the damsite the day before the explosion. Perhaps the most worrying aspect about the incident for the authorities was the expertise its perpetrators had displayed. At a press conference on April 20th, Mr Donald Johnstone, Chairman of the Clywedog Reservoir Authority, had to compliment the saboteurs on their technical know-how and ability.

Suddenly the mocking laughter directed at the Free Wales Army by some politicians and journalists began to sound hollow. It had begun to appear that the joke was on them...

Chapter Eight

IF THE DEMONSTRATION AT TRYWERYN had been the stone to start the threat of an avalanche of militant nationalism, then the bombing at Clywedog acted as the boulder which sent the whole mass crashing down the mountains. All over Wales groups of young men formed, styling themselves members of the Free Wales Army. The unknown initiator of the 'White Eagle' slogans had undoubtedly demonstrated a touch of genius, for it was exactly this combination of legend and romance which struck an answering chord in the Celtic soul. The further publicity given to Cayo Evans and the FWA as a result of Clywedog also brought into the movement a man who was to become a Commandant as famous, or notorious, as Cayo himself. His name was Denis Coslett.

In appearance Coslett was the classic type of fictional Welshman, short, dark-haired, lean and hard-bodied. His mannerisms exuding a highly charged nervous energy, and in speech fluent and excitable. His family also were of the classic fictional Welsh gender, producing famous rugby players and singers. Physically fearless, Coslett was always ready to meet force with force, with fist, boot, knife or gun. A hardline nationalist he wanted total separation for his country, and was an uncompromising anti-Communist.

Although his ancestors were of German origin, and he possessed an English grandfather, Denis Coslett identified completely with the land of his birth, to the extent of cymricising his name to Dafydd ap Coslett. An ex-infantryman who had served with the Royal Welch Fusiliers, he had also sailed the world as a seaman. Following his marriage he worked as a self-employed shotfirer in the small private coal mines that still survived independently after the nationalisation of the mining industry, until an accident cost him the sight of one eye and he was forced to work above the ground. His reasons for joining the FWA were expressed simply…

"The future of the Welsh language and nation looked bleak, and I believe that the FWA was born from a love of our language and our country. There was no possibility of achieving a free and independent Wales by constitutional means. It was for this reason we turned to a violent extreme nationalism. The politicians ignored Welsh aspirations, we had no stage to stand upon, and the only stage we could create was by threatening violence. As was proved later it was only after the creation of fear and chaos that the authorities called for a report on the existing constitution. I don't think this report would ever have come through the actions of the pacifist Plaid Cymru, because Westminster only ever laughed at them, before ignoring them.

"The Western Mail always accused the FWA of being anti-English, which I was most definitely not. If I was anti-English I would not endeavour to speak the English language which I love dearly, the same as I love my own language. But I will not betray the sanctity of my own language by becoming a monoglot English-speaking Welshman. I wanted the children of my country to have a full bilingual education, and the Welsh language to have a priority because it was then dying out fast… Dying out on the lips of Welsh schoolchildren.

"The first I knew about the existence of the Free Wales Army was reading the newspaper reports and articles following the Clywedog bombing. I had already formed a small group of my own, nothing to boast of, only four or five men, called the Welsh Republican Army, which we had kept in low profile. After reading about the FWA, I arranged a meeting with Cayo through nationalist friends, and his cousin brought him down here to Llanelli to meet me. His cousin, Eddie, had told him of my small group, and after a talk we decided to amalgamate and to work together. From that point on things moved quickly.

"In this area, Llanelli, Cydweli and the environs I didn't have to go looking for recruits. Once it was known that a column of the FWA was being organized here, they came looking for me. But to avoid any detriment to security I was fairly choosey about whom I accepted. I believe that we satisfied a deep-felt hunger in the hearts of the younger Welsh, because for years they had been waiting for someone to get up and make a stand for Wales.

"Of course, like every other country, we had our fair share of tap-room patriots. They were fine after half-past ten, stop tap. Plenty of fight in them then. But when you went to see them in the morning it was… 'Oohhhh noo, I don't think I can make it. Leave me out today… ' with their two lips all aquiver. I would think the proportion to be relied on was about one in a hundred. Fortunately there were enough hundreds coming forward for us to be able to find the ones. I trained my column on British Army lines, some drill and a lot of field training. They were mostly young lads in their late teens and early twenties, and not all were Welsh. There were kids with English and Irish parentage, even a German. I suppose you could term us the Llanelli Foreign Legion… "

Chapter Nine

A T A SERIES OF MEETINGS the area commandants of the expanding FWA attempted to work out the army organization, its tactics and long term strategy. The problem that was continually to bedevil them emerged almost at once. A collection of very diverse men, from vastly differing backgrounds and environments, their only common bond their shared love for Wales, they found it difficult to work equably in harness, or to accept one central commander. Allied to this was the traditional prejudice felt between North and South, between Welsh speaker and English speaker, between right wing and left wing political bias.

It was eventually decided that they would form a loosely federated army, each area commandant being solely responsible for his own column's training, logistics and operations. But that they would consult together frequently to try and avoid any clash of interest or overlap of action; and that they would accept certain general orders as binding upon them all. Finally they agreed upon and issued the following directive, which was to be the standard format for all units of the FWA…

BYDDIN RHYDDID CYMRU
NATIONAL MILITARY ORGANISATION OF WALES
OBJECT: (a) To organise, train, discipline and equip the manhood of Wales into a voluntary Military Organisation as a basis of a National Army of Free Wales, with sole allegiance to the Welsh nation and people. By organising such a force to be called the Free Wales Army, it would stand as a safeguard to the freedom of our homeland, and make all who think of encroaching on the

sovereignty of Wales wary of doing so.

(b) The Free Wales Army does not stand for terrorism or domination but for a policy of restraint unless the liberties of Wales and the Welsh people are threatened, as at Tryweryn, and if needed and it be the will of the people, then the FWA will do all possible to defend and fight for Wales.

(c) The FWA will not tolerate any sort of aggression or authority upon the Welsh nation and people by alien rulers and native quislings, and we shall endeavour to fulfil the following aims to the best of our abilities:

AIMS: (1) To free and defend Wales and the Welsh people from English rule, and from all other foreign interference, authority and aggression.

(2) To establish an independent Welsh Republic with sole allegiance to the Welsh people.

(3) To secure and maintain our rights and liberties, and to defend our heritage, the language, traditions and interests, economic and otherwise, common to all Welsh people.

(4) To unite under the flag of Free Wales, "Y Ddraig Goch, The Red Dragon", all able-bodied citizens of Wales in their country's service.

MEANS: What so ever be the will of our people.

ENLISTMENT FORM: (a) Before a volunteer is enlisted and signs this form, his name must be read out to fellow volunteers of his section. If no one objects to him joining then the volunteer will be required to fill in this form and swear the oath of allegiance.

(b) If his joining is objected to by another volunteer then it is up to the commanding officer to hear the reasons why, and to use his own discretion after consulting all the volunteers in the section. All objections are to be recorded together with the result of the final decision and the record kept at Brigade HQ.

(c) Membership in the FWA is free, but it would be appreciated that upon joining a volunteer contributes whatever he can afford towards Army funds... Enlistment form and money to be kept at Brigade HQ. Note. Where there is no Brigade Organisation, forms, money and records will be kept at Section level until such time as a Brigade or Battalion HQ has been established.

Enlistment Form as Below...

I, Christian and Surname, have read the objects and aims of the Army and agree with them, and desire to be enlisted for service in

Wales, or wherever duty calls as a volunteer in the FWA.

I promise to obey all rules and regulations as laid down in the Constitution of the Army, and follow all orders and directives as issued by the General Staff, Army Councils and Officers of the Army.

I pledge myself to a voluntary sense of discipline and I declare that in joining I accept the stated aims of the Army, and I further declare and promise that I will promote these aims to the best of my ability. I also realise that having enlisted I am eligible for service in the ranks of the Army for as long as I am needed at anytime and anywhere... Signature of Volunteer, and date.

OATH OF ALLEGIANCE: (a) Having enlisted and signed the necessary forms and being accepted into the Army, the volunteer must read out and sign this oath in the presence of his Commanding Officer and Section. The oath must be taken while the volunteer is holding the Flag of Free Wales, "Y Ddraig Goch".

OATH: I, give name, promise and affirm to dedicate my life to the cause of liberating my country from foreign domination; and that I will obey at all times the directives of the General Staff, Army Councils and Officers; and I will also uphold the discipline and honour of the Army.

I will honour and protect the sovereignty and rights of my country, people and flag, its language, traditions and culture.

I solemnly swear in the name of God, and in the name of our dead patriots, that I shall never reveal any secrets of our Army even if captured and tortured. If I betray this trust I shall deserve any punishment that may be meted out to me, and may eternal contempt cover me...

* * *

The Area Commandants also issued some basic rules and regulations on the organization of the Army:

RECRUITING: (a) All volunteers must be known, or vouched for before being admitted into Y FYDDIN. Anyone who approaches a known volunteer of Y FYDDIN and applies to join, or seeks information must not be told anything, only given details of object, aims and means. His name and address must be taken and given to the local section officer. He will then take steps to have the man vetted, i.e. antecedents, political views, character etc.

Anyone you may hear talking favourably of Y FYDDIN and expressing a desire to join, try and get his name and address, but do not openly admit that you are anything to do with Y FYDDIN unless you are a known volunteer. It will be the duty of a recruiting officer to contact these people — after they have been vetted by our intelligence men.

(b) Meetings/Training... Volunteers will attend all meetings and gatherings when and where required, in the appropriate dress for the occasion.

They will be expected to be prepared at short notice, and to leave work or other activities at any time during the day or night, and if necessary make their own way to any part of the country as commanded.

(c) General: All volunteers of Y FYDDIN are expected to be conversant with Army policy and shall be called upon to attend schools, and this will be a necessary part of officer and volunteer training.

The Format of the Army: The smallest unit of a Brigade shall be the Section of five men. This shall be the basis of Army organisation in any area. The Section will consist of men who live close together in one particular district, and who can be available at short notice for training or service.

Five sections will form one District Platoon; and four Platoons form one Area Company.

The training of a section will be basic guerrilla tactics, and basic drill, marching and weapon training. Emphasis must be placed on the men working as a team.

Uniforms and Equipment (Basic): All volunteers are expected to provide them- selves with a uniform and basic equipment. Combat uniform will consist of: Bottle-Green forage cap, shirt, neck scarf, combat jacket, denims, black boots, webbing belt. Basic Equipment: Trapper rucksack, water canteen, two side pouches, axe, knife. Ground sheet and blanket. Mess tins. Eating irons. This applies to all ranks. Badges and rank insignia will be issued by Commanding Officers.

To help with these instructions a picture of a fully equipped FWA soldier was mimeographed and distributed. There were also proposed dress uniforms of dark green jackets and black trousers.

FREE WALES ARMY
UNIFORM ALL RANKS
VOLUNTEER DAI EVANS. NR1 (CAPTAIN)

(A) RANK INSIGNIA (OFFICERS)

(B) COLLAR DOGS (OFFICERS)
(C) EPAULETTES (OFFICERS)
(D) OWAIN SHOULDER FLASHES
(E) DRAGON / WALES BADGE
(F) COMMAND FLASH
(G) BRIGADE UNIT FLASH
(H) CHEST FLASH
(I) BRASS EAGLE (ERIN)

(J) RANK FLASHES
    (SERGEANTS)
SERGEANTS, CORPORALS
& VOLUNTEERS 1ST CLASS

COMBAT UNIFORM
(ALL RANKS)
B/G FORAGE CAP.
GREEN SCARF.
B/G SHIRT.
B/G COMBAT JACKET
B/G TROUSERS
BLACK BOOTS
GRAY ANORAK SUIT
WEB BELT EQUIPAMENT
2 SIDE POUCHES
1 WATER CANTEEN
B/G TRAPPER RUCKSACK
BULLET POUCHES
GROUND SHEET.
BLANKET
AXE, KNIFE,
CAMPING PICK
AND SHOVEL.
ROPE.
BILLY CANS.
TIN CUP.

TIN PLATE
KNIFE & FORK.

*The fully
equipped
soldier of
the FWA*

GWENFRAN ARMY ORDERS (G.H.Q. POP AUGUST 1968)

70

*　*　*

It was much easier to issue directives and general instructions than to actually carry them out. To form any sort of efficient force needs money; and to arm, train, equip and expand that force it is necessary to have vast amounts of cash or credit to draw on. As Cayo Evans explained:

"It was once reported in the Irish newspapers that Cathal Goulding, the then Chief of Staff of the official Irish Republican Army, had given the FWA the guns held in store by the IRA. This was just not true. What happened was that an American arms company, ARMCO, offered us a sort of part exchange deal. Namely, they wanted us to buy the arms then in IRA hands, i.e. Thompson sub-machine-guns etc., using ARMCO as the intermediary and agent. With the money thus earned the IRA could then add to it and buy more modern and sophisticated weaponry from the company. ARMCO displayed as part of the sales pitch glossy coloured brochures featuring all types of weapons. Anything and everything was available, even tanks, aircraft and guided missiles. If the FWA had had the funds we could have equipped ourselves with everything needed in modern warfare. Unfortunately we never did have the cash for such transactions. We were a new army of volunteers and patriots; and as such never handled the vast sums of money available to well-entrenched organisations such as the IRA.

"Besides, it was never our intention to storm over the border in armoured cars and tanks. Ours was to be more of a war of propaganda, punctuated by acts of sabotage and shows of strength. Of course we wanted arms badly, and getting them presented a lot of problems. We bought, begged, borrowed, stole whatever we could get. War souvenirs, Granddad's revolver, rifles forgotten by the Home Guard, sporting rifles and shotguns, in fact anything that

71

could be fired. To be honest I think that any Folk museum would have been pleased to acquire some of our arms.

"However, if a man is taught to strip and maintain a stengun, should he later acquire a superior weapon, say an Uzzi, Karl Gustav or Sterling, he will find the basics of the gas and spring operated sub-machine-gun are all much the same. Automatic weapons have changed very little since the war, nor have other types. If a man gets sound basic knowledge with an old Webley 45 revolver, or learns to use a 1911 pattern Colt automatic, he will have no trouble in handling their modern counterparts. Teach a man to aim and fire an Enfield 303 and with a little thought and practice he can use an M16, SLR or Armalite. What we had to attempt to do with our volunteers was to inspire them with the same confidence and love of weapons that the average regular soldier possesses.

"Our uniforms were easier to obtain, and they also were for propaganda purposes as much as anything. We also believed that technically, if a man is caught in the act as it were, wearing a uniform which bears on its shoulder the name of his country in its national language, and its flag as a badge, then he is not a criminal but entitled to the treatment governing international warfare according to the laws of the Geneva Convention. But unfortunately in a fight of right against might, this is blatantly ignored by the more powerful forces.

"We bought our caps, combat jackets etc. from army-surplus stalls and shops, and dyed them bottle-green to avoid differences in shade. Once the badges and insignia were put on these uniforms there was no mistaking the army to which we belonged.

"The arms and uniforms were a very necessary factor in the field of propaganda. It is one thing to interview earnest idealists seeking peaceful means to attain their goals, but

Armoury of an FWA column

Weapon training, FWA style

quite another matter to interview armed and uniformed men prepared to fight to attain their goals. The open display of uniforms brought the Press and TV to us, and we made use of their interviews to put our aims and views across to the public. The media loved it, the establishment fell for it, and those who had scorned and poked fun, had another think. As the explosions increased, so we were there to give the reasons why, and each time to press home our arguments.

"Now of course at that time we had not sufficient organization or resources to initiate open guerrilla warfare. Although in the long term this was the obvious objective. What we had got the resources for however, was to instruct selected men in sabotage techniques, and the various methods of using those techniques... So at a remote farmhouse near Nebo in North Wales we set up a Bombing School... "

Chapter Ten

AMONG THE MEN who attended that bombing school was Lyn Ebenezer. Lyn was, he readily admits, not a fighting man, and had joined the FWA for reasons which differed from many of the hot-headed fervent patriots who thronged to it. He is a pleasant mannered, small statured man, with a French-style beard, blue eyes and an intellectual bent…

"My father was a staunch socialist, I was brought up on Aneurin Bevan at the breakfast table, in fact. Every morning listening to the radio news before I went to school I'd have a lesson in Socialism from my old man. He was a road-worker in Cardiganshire and he'd brought up 13 children; and with the help of a few friends managed to build his own house. He'd had to work damned hard all his life, and I can understand his alliance with the left wing of the Labour Party very well.

"Before I met Cayo I was a nationalist. I was aware that Wales wasn't getting a fair deal. I joined Plaid Cymru while I was in school, not as a staunch member or anything, but even joining Plaid Cymru then was a bit of a rebellious thing to do, it wasn't the done thing you see. I was only a member for a year or two. Then I met Cayo, completely by accident. I didn't know him before, but I'd heard of him, his wild escapades, like swimming the river in the middle of Winter, and riding a stallion through a pub etc. The FWA hadn't started then, so I was right in at the beginning.

"I remember the first time I met him. People had been telling me… "Duw! This fellow Cayo, he's a dangerous bugger! He's been up to all sorts of tricks." I was at a Young Farmers' meeting at Cross Inn and someone told me that Cayo was in the other room playing the accordion. So I went in, not knowing what to meet, half-afraid he might hammer me. Well, he was playing Irish music. Duw! I was straight at home. We became friends immediately. I've always been interested in Ireland, I don't know why, but I always have. I suppose I'm a bit of a romantic, I could never forget that handful of people in the 1916 rebellion challenging the might of the British Empire. But I can't say I'm anti-English, I don't hate the English as a race at all... I may hate some of them individually, but I also greatly like some of them individually. It's just that I'm pro-Wales, and I've always regarded us as a separate nation.

"After that first meeting Cayo and I started exchanging books about the Irish question. We were both very interested in the subject, and our friendship grew. He was then getting involved in the formation of the FWA. I remember going down to Cardiff with him just before Tryweryn was opened. I took different sides to Cayo in an argument that took place down there. He wanted to fight against the opening, and to form a fighting movement. I just wanted a movement to protest, to show people that we objected to what was being done to our country.

"But it wasn't so much the movement, as Cayo, who intrigued me. In fact no matter what his politics might have been I would have wanted to be friends with him. He was everything that I wasn't. He'd travelled the world, and could talk of places I'd only read of. He introduced me to another world I never knew existed. Like horses, for example. Even though I was brought up in the country I'd never mixed in the horse world, the dealers, the Romanies, the tinkers etc. Cayo was always mixing with people like the Gypsy types that I'd been taught to sort of look down on. They weren't supposed to be nice people at all. I was brought up to the chapel, very respectable. This was all a new world to me. It wouldn't have mattered which side Cayo had taken, I would have gone with him. He was the sort of friend I'd never had. A character completely out of the ordinary.

"At the time, when the FWA went into uniform, I thought it was great fun, the novelty of it attracted me. But when I got drawn deeper into it, I saw that it wasn't just a game. That they were aiming at something concrete. For the first time in my life it brought me into close contact with the police, and on the opposing side at that, to make it worse…"

A man named Major Thompson, an ex-British officer, owned a farm at a place known as Blaenpennal. Cayo Evans knew the man well, and in return for the services of one of Cayo's stallions the major gave him a Webley 38 revolver and ammunition. Since most of the West Wales column already had a gun of some sort, except for Lyn Ebenezer, Cayo gave him the gun one night at his home village of Pontrhydfendigaid. The ammunition was wrapped in an old army sock of the major's. After the bombing at Clywedog the police, knowing of Lyn Ebenezer's connections with Cayo Evans and the FWA, came to search his house.

"… What happened was that the Clywedog affair had just occurred, and Cayo had given me the gun some days previously. I'd never had a gun in my life, or even fired one for that matter. I took this one out into the fields a few times and tried to shoot a rabbit, and couldn't hit a thing. I couldn't even see where my shots were striking. So in the end I gave up, and put the gun in my drawer in the bedroom, together with the sockful of rounds and a picture of Kevin Barry, all my treasures, as it were.

"The night of Clywedog I was at a dance in Felin Fach, I couldn't have been much further away from the place. Well, the police came to question me, although they knew I'd had nothing to do with Clywedog. These were local CID. There had been a nationalist meeting some nights before in Bont at which there had been a lot of fiery talk and a raffle for a huge Celtic banner that Tony Lewis had made. I remember it was won by a farmer who was later pulled in by the law for possessing a rebel flag. Anyway, the police thought this meeting was very sinister, although it had been quite open, and they were keeping a close eye on the village.

"When they came to my house I had a letter in my pocket from Tony Lewis, a sinister-style revolutionary one with all sorts of code thing in it which I didn't understand myself. So I knew that if the police found that, it would immediately give them something to be suspicious about. Three of them arrived, and while one was questioning me the others searched the room. Then the one in charge said. 'Go up and search his bedroom.'… I suddenly remembered that I'd got the gun and ammo up there. I was really scared, I'll tell you. I thought, 'God, this is it! This is it! They'll have me now! I'll get ten years for this!'

"So up I went, as quick as I was able.

"The bloke was searching the cupboard where there was a very old gun which didn't work, and had been there for years. I thought that even if they spotted that one, I'd be in trouble. Anyway, the gun was right in front of him and he missed it. But I knew that he couldn't possibly miss the one in the drawer, it was right on top of everything else. So I told the bloke. 'I might as well help you. The sooner you're out of here the better for everyone concerned.'

"My heart was pounding so hard I was sure he'd hear it thumping. I took the drawer out and put it on the bed, threw a coat over it, and slipped the gun and ammo out of the drawer and shoved them into my jacket pockets. I tipped the drawer's contents out onto the bed and invited him to look through them, which he did. When he told me I could put everything back, I managed to slip the gun back into the drawer, but couldn't get rid of the sockful of ammunition.

"In the meantime they'd searched my mother's bedroom as well. She was bed-ridden, but they moved her so they could search the bed. Never mind, they had to do it, I suppose, but my brothers and sisters were very angry about it when they heard. We went back downstairs and they were going through the door when the bloke in charge stopped dead. 'Hold on a minute,' he told his mates. 'We haven't searched his pockets.' Duw! My heart stopped cold!

"They found the letter and they found the sock of bullets. So they took me into Aberystwyth for further questioning. It was the old treatment, keeping me awake all night, and having men come past me with gelignite, fuses etc, and saying loudly. 'Ohh we've got Cayo Evans. We've found all this at his place.'

"But there was I with nothing to tell them. I really didn't know anything. I hadn't been near Clywedog, and I hadn't got the slightest idea who'd done it. When they asked me about the bullets, I could only tell them that I couldn't remember how the hell they'd got into my pocket. Since they knew that Cayo had bullets because he'd collected some guns as a hobby in the past, I said, 'Perhaps Cayo came to the house and left them there. I can't remember now.'

"In the meantime the police went to my girlfriend's home and told her that I'd confessed to bombing Clywedog, and asked her what other things she could tell them to make it easier on me. The poor girl didn't know what they were on about.

"They let me go at six o'clock in the morning. I rushed back and got the gun and gave it to a publican I knew who had an antique arms collection. He told me some time later that he'd handed it to the police on the arms amnesty for the county. I was too scared about it to worry, I'll tell you…"

Even before Lyn had calmed down from his near escape, his friendship with Cayo Evans was to bring him another fright. He was then just breaking into the field of journalism by acting as a part-time freelance reporter for various local newspapers.

"I was on my way down the Black Lion in Pontrhydfendigaid for a Saturday morning pint, and I met Cayo sitting outside the pub in his car. 'Jump in,' he said, 'I've got a good story for you today. You'll get a headline out of it.'

"We picked two more of the boys from our column up, Osborne and Pete Goginan. Off we went up North to a poultry farm. There was a lot of boys from various columns already up there, but there was I, all innocence, not knowing what the hell was going on. Suddenly I was introduced to this man who was the 'Bomb-Maker'… Well! I was really scared this time, almost messing my pants! I've never been a brave fellow in my life, and this was it. I thought, 'Christ Almighty! We'll be caught now for sure.'

"When we were settled for the night a cylinder was brought into the room where some of us were sleeping and put on the dresser. It was a bomb. They just shoved it casually on the dresser, and I couldn't sleep a wink all night. The only thing that gave me any comfort I remember, was Dai Bomber's cigar. The only thing that gave me a bit of strength through the night was this bloody cigar puffing and blowing like a Vesuvius. I kept telling myself there couldn't be anything to worry about if he could smoke so close to the bomb.

"We got up next morning and I was very nervous, expecting the police to come charging through the farmyard and into the house at any moment. Off we went across the fields, the bomb was stuck up on a wall, and the fuse lit. Whoosh! A column of smoke and nothing bloody happened.

FWA bomb school

Not a bloody stone moved… I'll never forget the Bomb-Maker's comment… 'Ah well, back to the fucking drawing board.'

"I was sweating, I'll tell you. I was bloody worried, man! Blowing up walls on the side of Snowdonia, not half a mile from the main road??? While we were waiting for another demonstration we were issued with the newly printed FWA membership and identity cards. I'll tell you I was bloody reluctant to take mine. I didn't think my nerves would stand much more …"

The Bomb-Maker, an old-time Welsh Republican hardliner, made no more errors. For the rest of that day and the day following using cigar-cases as bomb containers, he demonstrated to his eager pupils the effects of different types of explosives and powder. He also gave lectures on how to manufacture bombs, and how to obtain maximum results from different types of charges. A briefing on incendiary devices, and how to create either fire or smoke was also included.

There was an engineer present who lectured on the weak points of various structures, and where to place the bombs to obtain maximum and minimum damage results on different fabrics, i.e. brick, stone, metal, wood, etc.

These lessons of this brief seminar would not be fully utilised by the FWA until some months later. By then, however, the climate of opinion in Wales had hardened on both sides, and the Government at Westminster was to set up a special squad of detectives and intelligence men to deal with a situation that unless strong measures were taken, threatened to escalate into virtual civil war…

Chapter Eleven

Because of his great interest in Irish affairs Cayo Evans had kept in touch with the Irish Republican friends he had made while serving in the British Army. He had visited Ireland many times and had come to know personally several high-ranking IRA officers. Immediately after the Clywedog bombing he conceived of yet another brilliant publicity coup, which through his IRA contacts he hoped to arrange.

The Fiftieth anniversary of the 1916 Easter Day Rising was due to be commemorated and a great parade was to be staged in Dublin, in which revolutionary independence organisations from all over the world were to be invited to take part. Cayo Evans went to work and soon the Free Wales Army received a cordial invitation from Sinn Fein to become one of those participating organisations. Plaid Cymru was also to be represented in Dublin, but their invitation came from official Irish Government sources.

For Cayo Evans the Dublin parade was one of the highspots of his life. The British Special Branch had also been alerted to what was to take place however…

"Once I'd received the invitation from Sinn Fein, I spread the word to all columns of the FWA that as many of their men as possible should try and get to Dublin to march with us of the West Wales column. The anniversary of the Uprising conveniently coincided with the Wales/Ireland rugby match in Dublin, and several boatloads of Welsh rugby supporters were travelling over to Ireland for the match, so it was easy for our boys to mingle unobtrusively with the crowds on the docks. The reason for us not wanting to be seen leaving was a simple one. Through a friendly source connected with the Welsh Regional Crime squads we had been tipped off that the Special Branch would be keeping us under surveillance in Ireland, to watch whom we contacted there. It must be remembered that the British and the Irish Special Branches co-operate with each other in acting against hardline groups such as the IRA and the FWA.

"One of our sympathisers who worked on the Fishguard docks saw myself and some of my friends in the crowd and came to warn us that in the dock police office there were some Special Branch men disguised as long-haired hippy types, waiting to go on board with us. We were able to get a good look at these lads with the help of our sympathiser, so we knew who they were. Since they would be crossing with us we anticipated that there might be a little difficulty at Rosslare, where we would disembark. So we distributed our flags, caps, badges etc. among some helpful rugby supporters for them to take off the boat for us.

"I remember it was raining when we reached Ireland, so I strapped my accordion onto my back and wore my overcoat cloak-style over it to protect it from the rain. When I was coming down the gangplank a couple of nuns suddenly rushed up to me.

" 'Och, ye poor soul!' One kept saying. 'Leave us help yez down. Take it nice and easy now, there's a good man.'

"It wasn't until they each took one of my arms that I realised the kind-hearted creatures thought I was a crippled hunchback.

"The hippy Special Branch moved quickly, because within a few moments of stepping onto the quayside, myself and the other FWA men with me were politely requested by Irish plainclothes detectives to step into a convenient office.

They questioned us at length about our antecedents, and why we had come to Ireland. We insisted that we were rugby supporters, but it was only after a thorough body-search that they let us go with a warning to keep out of mischief while we were in Ireland. We still had the problem of the hippies to deal with. The train goes from Rosslare to Wexford, and then on to Dublin. Our helpers gave us back our gear once the train was on its way, and we checked the whereabouts of the Special Branch undercover men. They were separated, one each in the coaches before and behind us, and one at the end of our coach. We waited until the train was pulling out of the Wexford station, then simply jumped out onto the platform. As it rattled off out of the station three long-haired heads popped out of the windows glaring back at us. We put our caps on and waved them goodbye. If looks could kill none of us would have survived that moment.

"That first day was spent on the Wexford waterfront. People were very interested in our badges and flags, and showed us warm hospitality. I was playing the accordion in one pub and a bedridden old man was carried downstairs to listen to me. At his request I played *Boulovogue* and he started to weep. I could only hope that he was crying because he was a patriot, and not because he was a musician.

"In Dublin all the FWA men met up. The city was packed, I should think every derelict rebel in the world was there that week. Most of the FWA were staying in Morans Hotel, about twelve men to a double bed, it was so crowded.

"The actual march was one of the proudest moments of my life. Scores of our boys from all over Wales had managed to get to Dublin. There were two big separate parades. The Free State parade, which the Plaid Cymru delegation marched with, routed for the Kilmainan Jail; and our parade, the Republican. The Flag parties of each contingent led, with the rank and file following the massed banners. I felt tremendously proud to be carrying the Red Dragon that day. The Irish Republican Army with their pipeband and the old veterans headed the procession. We came behind them and had a terrific reception from the crowds of spectators when they saw the Welsh flag. The Breton Liberation Movement followed us with their black and white flags, then the Flemish, the Vec Mannin (Manx Independence movement), Irish Americans, Cornish Republicans of the Mebyon Kernow (Sons of Cornwall), French Canadians, Scottish Liberation Army, there seemed to be dozens of different groups on parade. There was even a bunch of Glasgow Celtic football supporters marching behind their own flag, a tricolour with an Irish Shamrock centred — there's little doubt about that club's political loyalties.

"Our route was from the Custom House to Glasnevin Cemetery. It stirred my conscience to see the Easter Lily wreaths laid on the graves of the dead Irish patriots there. A very tall, red-haired Belfast Irishman, with a plug of cottonwool in his ear and a revolver in a shoulder holster pointed out to me the graves of his relatives, and the grave of Sir Roger Casement. When the bugler played the Last Post I was near to tears myself. Here, all about me was the proof that men reviled in their day by world opinion as rebels, had been prepared to give their lives for their cause, and for their dream of a free nation…"

The Irish newspapers featured the FWA contingent in pictures and interviews, as did James Nicholson of the British *Daily Sketch*; and the representatives of the other Freedom Movements present took notice that a new force had arisen with aims similar to their own: to gain independence for a minority people almost submerged by a vast alien majority.

The Plaid Cymru delegation had been instructed to avoid the FWA; nevertheless a sizeable number of their younger element had in fact marched with the Green Caps.

*The Red Dragon
on parade in Dublin*

Once the solemnities of the anniversary were completed Dublin gave itself over to enjoyment; and the FWA men were happy to wander through its pubs and streets, mingling with all the colourful characters that the occasion had drawn there. Denis Coslett in full uniform was quick to aid the street-sellers of the Republican newspaper, the *United Irishman*. Taking a bundle from one of them he stopped passers-by and badgered them to buy. He wouldn't accept less than half a crown for copy, and if asked for change remonstrated with pained amazement. "Do you begrudge a few extra pence for the Cause?" Few did, and the street-sellers were happy to receive the large amount of money he had gained for them.

In a square they came upon an ancient Irish-American, a veteran of the early fighting in 1916. He was on his knees staring up at a statue of Daniel O'Connel and shouting fiercely,

"Daniel O'Connel, can you hear me? Can you hear me, O'Connel? Are you listening to what I'm telling ye, Daniel O'Connel?"

He insisted on taking the FWA boys to a bar, where he claimed to have shot two 'Tans' during the troubles, and once there re-enacted the whole drama that had taken place, much to the delight of the local drunks. After this, he took everyone back to the Gresham Hotel where he had a room, and after ringing room-service for drinks made them all hide in ambush positions behind the furniture. The old man was so carried away with excitement that when the waiter appeared with the tray of drinks he sprang on him and tried to throttle him, shouting out that the poor man was a traitor to the Fenian Cause. Fortunately one of the Welshmen was able to catch the bottle of whisky as it fell with the tray, while the others rescued the waiter and pacified the veteran.

One young FWA volunteer, nicknamed Enrico for his

Mediterranean type looks, found the local brew a little more potent than his customary half pint of cider. He became convinced that they were in Dublin to re-enact the storming of the GPO and kept asking plaintively, "When will they give us the guns?" Later in the night he was to wake up his sleeping companions by jumping up in a nightmare screaming out, "No, don't shoot me! Don't shoot me!" He also woke up half the hotel, and the guests took a lot of convincing that no actual murder attempt was taking place.

The wild celebrations continued through the return journey. On the St. David ferry which ran a special trip from Dun Laoghaire to Fishguard, Denis Coslett and others replaced the poopmast Union Jack with the Welsh Red Dragon, then announced over the loud-speaker system that the FWA had taken the ship, and were heading her towards the Welsh colony in Patagonia. The hundreds of rugby supporters cheered wildly and waited enthusiastically for the change of course. The ship's captain, a Welsh-speaker himself, took it in good part and shared a friendly drink with the FWA men. Denis Coslett finished by taking a collection among the passengers for the Army funds, and was given enough to be able later to buy an old motorbike and sidecar for his column's use.

*   *   *

These were exciting days for the young leaders of the FWA. Its strength snowballed beyond all their expectations, every week bringing its quota of would-be recruits and letters of support. Many of the would-be recruits were university and college students, but as one Commandant pointed out to the Army Council: "These students are all die-hard nationalists, but they don't want to be in any danger of dying. They're all right to do a bit of painting on walls and bridges, and to shout their heads off at demonstrations from the safe rear of the crowd. But when the going gets a little rough, they don't want to know."

The truth of his words was already apparent to the FWA commanders, and student recruits were normally kept well on the fringes of the organisation.

Like all rebel armies everywhere the rough, weird and crackpot elements came hovering about them like moths to a flame. Crackpots such as the South Walian who was forever phoning up newspapers and different official bodies claiming that he was a General of the FWA and threatening to bring death and destruction on all and sundry by bizarre means. He eventually became such an embarrassment that he had to be warned off. There were the drunken brawlers who when arrested for causing disturbances would say that they belonged to the FWA, and would get the 'boys' down to blow up the police station unless they were released immediately. Even a weird religious fanatic who claimed that the FWA would bring Armageddon to Cardiff, and that they were the chosen instrument of God's will.

Because of the virtual autonomy of the different columns it became more difficult as the organisation expanded for the senior commandants such as Evans and Coslett to personally monitor all that was happening in areas other than their own. So they were forced to bear with the publicity resulting from an occasion when some FWA volunteers stripped the lead from the roof of the Bishop's Palace at Llandâf and sold it, then pocketed the money. When the police caught them they claimed that their criminal profits had been used for FWA funds, and that they had committed their offence as an act of war.

The senior commandants refused to condone this type of conduct, but they could and did condone the light-hearted pranks indulged in by some of their members, such as a man known by his nickname, Goginan. Squat and plump, with a large head and full spade beard, he possessed a magnificently sonorous voice, and had won many prizes for poetry recitals at the Eisteddfods, and for his very talented acting. He was a lay-preacher who at one time intended to enter the ministry, but he became addicted to strong drink, and the bottle increasingly took precedence over the preaching until he was eventually barred from the pulpit. The main reason for this ban was because during the referendum campaign for Sunday pub-opening in Cardiganshire, Goginan, an uncannily accurate mimic, toured the district in the chapel's loud-speaker van urging the local people to vote in favour of Sunday opening. As if this were not wicked enough in the eyes of the Chapel Elders, Goginan added insult to injury by imitating the local minister's voice while uttering his perjorations in favour of drink over the loudspeaker. He succeeded so well that when next the unfortunate preacher — a strict teetotaller — ascended his pulpit, howls of angry abuse from the congregation greeted his appearance.

After his expulsion Goginan's favourite practice was to travel around the various chapels watching the ranting preachers and memorising their voices, mannerisms and pet sermons. Every time he was drunk, which was frequently, he would then mount a convenient bar-stool or table and give out the latest sermon he had heard, complete with mimicry. His favourite sermon was the story of Moses leading the Children of Israel out from bondage. He would dwell long and movingly on their sufferings, and describe with emotion throbbing in his voice the cruel Pharaoh of Egypt pursuing them with his chariots across the opened Red Sea. The grand finale was Moses causing the sea to close upon the wicked Egyptians while shouting in a voice like thunder: "AND ARSEHOLES TO YOU TOO, PHARAOH!"

Cayo Evans himself could not resist the temptation of taking a rise out of the letter-writers to the local press who would indignantly demand of the editors the reasons why the police did not arrest the FWA men for parading in uniform. He invented a character named the Reverend Idwal Lloyd-Price, and sent letters in his name to the same newspapers quoting fictitious extracts from the United Nations Bill of Human Rights and the Geneva Convention in justification of the uniforms and parades. Sometimes the correspondence would continue for weeks with anti and pro-reverend readers joining in. Any letters sent to the Reverend at his home address presented a problem to the local postman, who knew that it was a ruined cottage in the village of Silian with a tree growing out of its chimney.

Another side effect of the publicity the FWA received was encountered with mixed feelings by the Commandants. This was the aphrodisiac influence the idea of rebellion seemed to have on certain types of women. Both Denis Coslett and Cayo Evans received several wildly passionate letters from female admirers, who begged the commandants to father rebel babies upon them. The commandants' wives quickly put a stop to that sort of offered aid.

These lighter moments helped to compensate for the many frustrations the FWA faced. As Denis Coslett put it, "At times it was easy to lose heart. We had no finance, no decent transport, no modern weapons, we had nothing except our faith in a Free Wales."

The frustrations sometimes bordered on the farcical. On one occasion an urgently needed box of gelignite had to be collected and moved from South Wales to Cayo Evans' area. His own car was being repaired so Cayo was forced to borrow an ancient wreck of a van, brakeless, exhaustless, engine coughing, doors hanging loose. After working with his horses all day and evening, he then drove south in the van. The night was a stormy one, rain pouring down and winds buffeting the mountains.

The pick-up point was at a remote crossroads to which Denis Coslett had been given a lift by a long-distance transport driver who was a fringe member of the FWA.

Some five miles distance from the rendezvous one of the van's front wheels spun off, and the vehicle crashed grindingly to a halt, its bonnet buried in a ditch. There was no spare wheel, and without a torch the night was too dark for Cayo Evans to find the missing wheel. So, with the weather tormenting him he made his way on foot to where Denis Coslett, sheltered shiveringly in the hedgerows, was waiting. Together they carried the box of gelignite back to the stranded van, then searched for and found an isolated farmhouse, and persuaded the farmer to come out with his tractor and pull the van back onto the road. With the aid of the tractor's headlights they were able to locate the missing wheel, and eventually to refit it. Then, at three o'clock in the morning, cold, hungry, drenched to the skin, they were finally able to start back to their respective homes and the day's work that awaited them.

Chapter Twelve

KEITH GRIFFITHS, Welsh name Gethin ap Iestyn, black-eyed, black-haired, stocky and volatile, was described at his trial by Detective Chief Inspector John Owen Evans of the Special Branch, as a "great propagandist, who throws ideas into the air like little balls." Mr Tasker Watkins QC and prosecutor of the Free Wales Army called him, "a man wedded to the use of violence." Keith Griffiths merely regarded himself as a staunch patriot...

"My family wasn't nationalist though. This is one of the failures of Wales in that someone becomes a nationalist, but doesn't necessarily pass it on to their children as they do in Ireland, where there are hundreds of traditionally nationalist families. Here in Wales one person in the family can become a nationalist, but it ends with him.

"I was born in Merthyr, my father's family were from Gilfach and were all miners. My mother's family also had been hardrock miners for generations. We moved to Bridgend when I was seven, just me and my brother in family. I went to school in the Bridgend area, ending up at Pencoed Secondary Modern. I became a nationalist at the age of fourteen. It started with the slow rejection of the way history was taught; and a consciousness developing in Welsh language lessons, where we'd take as much mick out of the teacher as possible because we didn't want to learn Welsh. Over the following years this slowly growing rejection of British Empire history increasingly meshed with the question in my mind of just why was I taking the mick out of this Welsh teacher? Then one day at school, quite by chance, I came across a Welsh history book for the first time in my life, which gave the story of Welsh history mainly in medieval times, and that started to convince me that there was something wrong.

"As I rejected the English history and read my own I began to feel that I'd been robbed of something. Cheated, by not being informed of the other side of the coin, for it's so very easy to become English, speaking their language, and looking like them. So I started treading the road towards nationalism. A friend of mine was going the same way, and he said that he'd heard a Plaid Cymru radio broadcast, when it was an unofficial pirate one. This was in 1962 and it spurred us on a bit, even to painting slogans on the school walls. After that nothing much came of it because being on the young side we couldn't get in touch with nationalist organisations. I left school and ended up working in a textile factory in Somerset. While there I managed to get in touch with Plaid Cymru and joined them.

"Through their newspaper I learned that they were holding a big summer conference in Fishguard in 1964, so packed up my job and went to Fishguard. I worked on a farm there for six months until the conference began. At the conference I met Tony Lewis, whom I was to work very closely with in the future. But in those days I was involved solely with the Plaid, but I did get into trouble with the police in Fishguard for pulling down Union Jacks and bunting at a local fête. A Plaid Cymru official came to the station and got me out. Although Plaid Cymru were not militant they had not yet become so acceptable to the Establishment, and there was a very strong younger element and a thriving young nationalist association incorporated in the party.

"Later I went to a Celtic League conference in Bangor. The Celtic League is an organisation of nationalists from all the Celtic centres of the world, Ireland, Wales, Scotland, Brittany, Isle of Man, Cornwall etc. and it has a different committee for each country. In the League magazine the Irish tend to write about the armed struggle, and the Welsh about the cultural struggle, which perhaps illustrates the difference between our two nations. At that conference in Bangor I noticed how our Welsh Language Society people were more active and closely bound together because of their shared language.

"That's another sad thing about Wales, there is no middle ground. In Ireland or Scotland if you don't speak Gaelic but only English, still you are not taken solely into the English sphere of influence, you still have a music and a culture to step into. In Wales you can only step into the English influence. The failure of the Language Society is that they say, 'Well, if you're not Welsh speaking, that's it, you're out!'

"I, and a few others thought we must attempt something in South Wales to rally people towards nationalism, but obviously being English speakers it couldn't be done through the Welsh language. I'd kept in touch with Tony Lewis since the Fishguard conference, and together we formed an organisation called the Anti-Sais (English) Front, which wasn't anti-English as such, but anti-Anglicisation, and we took much of our inspiration for it from developments in the Flemish areas of Belgium, and from the French-Canadians of Quebec, where the militancy was just emerging strongly. We tried to make the Front patriotic but not on the Welsh language alone. Hence we wore a lot of badges and sweatshirts with slogans on them. When the FWA slogans began to appear some of our members styled themselves Free Wales Army as well.

"Unfortunately I missed the Tryweryn demonstration. The coach never showed up, the lifts Were bad, and by the time I reached Bala all the nationalists had gone home. I ended up spending a very uncomfortable night in a ticket-collector's box in Machynlleth. I think that Tryweryn really got the whole thing going, because at this time people like Harri Webb and Meic Stephens were writing patriotic songs and overall there was a strong surge of patriotism… "

Keith Griffiths and Tony Lewis were more politically minded than their fellow patriots Cayo Evans and Denis Coslett; and thought that they could serve the cause better by forming an independent political pressure group on the fringes of Plaid Cymru, than by becoming just another military column of the FWA. So they were to publicly disassociate themselves from the FWA in July 1966, but continued to work with them both publicly and privately, particularly after their virulent clashes with the Plaid Cymru hierarchy which occurred a little later. As Keith Griffiths explained:

"I was always more interested in the political side of things. Certainly I supported the Free Wales Army, because it could be said to symbolise a Welsh military manhood. We've always had this nonsense of Welsh pacifism foisted onto us. This is a lie, because the medieval Welsh society was a militarist society based on warrior castes, the Teulu, the armed bands of the Princes, every man a warrior. I believed basically as did the Israelis in the Haganah, that the nationalist movement had to have a military wing to act as a threat. Not necessarily to go into action then and there, but to be there as an existing threat; and at the same time to be used as a propaganda weapon to direct people into useful tasks during times of crisis, like Aberfan, for instance. Instead of the British Army coming in, the Free Wales Army could do so.

"Anyway, Tony and myself then went ahead and formed the *Patriotic Front*, mostly recruiting from the young English speaking Welsh people that the Language Society and Plaid

Cymru had left in a void. We created a new uniform, green sidecap, black trousers, khaki shirts, and a new emblem, three gold rays of light radiating from the top of a crown, based on the story of God's message, Love, Truth and Justice, which we took for our motto. Initially we hoped to be incorporated into the Plaid Cymru to cater for the more militant, or positive elements within the party… "

All this activity, this bubbling ferment of re-awakened Welsh nationalism was suddenly, and quite startlingly brought to the attention of the recently returned to power Labour Government at Westminster, when, in a by-election at Caerfyrddin in July 1966, a firmly held Labour seat was captured by the Plaid Cymru candidate. The party president, Gwynfor Evans doubled his previous share of the poll and became the first member of Plaid Cymru to sit in the House of Commons.

Tony Lewis was convinced that it was the resurgent militancy of Welsh nationalism that won the seat for the Plaid.

"… The Plaid hierarchy were still too airy-fairy and living in the land of the Methodist preacher and schoolteacher, so it really wasn't a party of the common, ordinary working people. As much as the hierarchy tried to deride direct action, yet it worked. When Clywedog dam was blown up and the crane and cables destroyed, within seven days a thousand people had joined Plaid Cymru. I know this because I was in the Plaid office and they showed me the figures. They joined because of the publicity generated by this explosion and by the Free Wales Army. Because people thought, 'Things are happening!'

"Our own new organisation, the Patriotic Front, gained strength very quickly. The main branch and the headquarters were at Cwmbran, but several other branches came into being. In Aberdâr the branch badge was a black diamond to represent their coal fields. In the Rhondda they took the 'War Axe of Lord Rhys', as their badge. Gethin (Keith Griffiths) and myself opened a club in Cwmbran called the *Patriot's Rest*; we thought this would be a good thing because all the other parties had their clubs dotted around, and we wanted the same thing as a focal point for nationalism.

"After Gwynfor Evans got into Parliament a Plaid Cymru conference met at Maesteg. As many Patriotic Front members as possible went to this conference, many of us in uniform. In fact the entire front row of the audience was composed of our uniformed members. Gwynfor Evans liked this and congratulated us on our efforts in the by-election. We decided that same day, that because Gwynfor was so impressed with us, we would not do anything in a military way, but would remain purely political."

As the poet once said, the road to Hell is paved with good intentions. Some of the more elderly zealots of Plaid Cymru were not happy with the 'Young Turks' of the Patriotic Front. The elders looked with a jaundiced eye at the success of the club, *The Patriot's Rest*, and accused its organisers of using the profits made by the folk-song evenings and similar events, for purposes other than Plaid Cymru funds. In fact the Patriotic Front were barely covering the running costs of the club, but a couple of Plaid stalwarts in Cwmbran called in the police and demanded that Tony Lewis turn over his financial records for scrutiny. The acrimonious bickerings went on, and on, and on, tempers were lost and insults exchanged. Relations rapidly worsened between the militants and the party hierarchy and at the Plaid conference at Dolgellau in August 1966, both the Patriotic Front and the Free Wales Army were outlawed by Plaid Cymru. Owain Williams of Tryweryn fame was also expelled from the Plaid for being the Vice-President of the Patriotic Front. The expulsion was laughed at by Owain

Williams, who had in fact already resigned from the party. As he queried, "How can a non-member be expelled?"

This Dolgellau conference initiated the open verbal warfare between Plaid Cymru and the extremist groups which was to rage bitterly through the coming years. The party's Vice-president, Mr E.G. Millward, the one-time firebrand who had helped organise the demonstration of the Welsh Language Society at Aberystwyth in 1963, fired the opening shots, declaiming dramatically:

"I have long tired of the pranks of this little army, the FWA, playing with the subject of freedom for Wales. It needs to be said once and for all, that our party has nothing to do with either the FWA or PF and if they have any sympathisers among our members this motion gives branches immediate powers to expel them.

"There is no room and never has been in a responsible political party for these 'Paper Tigers'. Their place is in their own private cloud cuckoo land. All Wales is sick of these effete publicity seekers… "

Mr Barrie Cox of Cwmbran eagerly followed his party superiors' line, blaming FWA activities for losing Plaid Cymru considerable support in local elections. He then laid sinister information before his enthralled audience, imparting the following items… "The FWA are better organised than many think, and are tools of organisations outside Wales. We know they have been in contact with various Fascist movements!" He went on to tell of the FWA's "… knife carrying, LSD and psychedelic activities… "

Needless to say, after these blood-curdling revelations the resolution to outlaw the FWA was carried overwhelmingly by the delegates.

Cayo Evans, spokesman for the "Knife carrying, LSD, and psychedelic Paper Tigers" answered reporters' questions about the resolution with tongue in cheek sadness: "We have never condemned Plaid Cymru as such. All we have condemned is their incapacity of doing anything other than passing resolutions which get them nowhere."

*   *   *

Another event was to take place in September which the FWA were making full use of to create publicity for their aims, and to goad the authorities. The eight million pounds cost Severn Bridge was to be opened by Her Majesty, Queen Elizabeth. The bridge had been a source of some contention during its construction and certain Welsh nationalists were bitterly opposed to it since they saw this new road link as a move to increase the English domination of South Wales. One small FWA column had attempted to disrupt the completion of the bridge, but their efforts were ineffectual, as one volunteer remembers...

"We did some military-style training in our small group and decided to try and do a bit of damage around the Severn Bridge. We couldn't try to blow the bridge because we knew nothing about explosives in our column, but we tried to carry out symbolic acts of sabotage, sand in engines and generators etc. Then when the final section had gone into place and the dais and everything was ready for the Queen, we set off one day to see if we could do anything to disrupt the preparations for the opening ceremony. One group went across the ferry, which was still open, one group went by rail around the Aust, and a third group went to the Chepstow side. We intended if nothing else to burn the dais and anything that was combustible. But by the time we arrived the place had filled up with soldiers, and there were security fences and dogs. The amazing thing is that the soldiers were not allowed to leave the bridge and come onto Welsh soil..."

It's fair to point out that the soldiers were there to guard the bridge, and not patrol Welsh soil.

A journalist, John Roberts, enabled Cayo Evans to push the FWA again into the headlines when he interviewed the West Wales commandant on behalf of the popular *Tit Bits* magazine shortly before the bridge's opening following a spate of letters and phone calls attributed to the FWA which threatened to blow the bridge up on the day of the ceremony. Roberts' article, beneath the headline, *There'll be a Welcome in the Hillsides*, featured a large photograph of an armed Cayo and two lieutenants guarding their banner. It also quoted Cayo as saying that the hotheads in his column could not always be kept in check, and anything might be expected to happen on the day the Queen came to the Severn.

'Atticus', the columnist of the prestigious Sunday Times, used the same photograph for his own interview with Cayo Evans, which was rather more muted in tone, but said basically the same things. The Gloucestershire police played down any ideas that the FWA were causing them undue anxiety. Chief Superintendent Albert Carter stated, "We have kept watch on the bridge with due regard to the trouble these people have caused in Wales. Whenever there is a big project like the bridge, some crank wants to blow it up. But we'll have plain-clothes men sprinkled in the crowd at the opening, just in case."

The promised sprinkle of plain-clothes men abruptly altered to a positive downpour of armed soldiers, police and dogs as a round-the-clock security guard was mounted some days before the opening, which was to be maintained for some time after it also. Despite the almost shamefaced denials of the authorities, it seemed that the threats of FWA action had had effect. In event the only thing blown up was the plaque commemorating the opening ceremony, which the FWA destroyed some time later.

It appeared that once more Cayo Evans had demonstrated an uncanny grasp of media-utilisation to force

Military guard on the Severn Bridge

The young Keith Griffiths and members of the Patriotic Front

the authorities into panic-reaction, and to embarrass the Establishment politicians of Wales. The media flocked to Cayo Evans for dramatic and colourful material, and he gave them a feast of such. It was little wonder that when asked yet again about the Free Wales Army, Gwynfor Evans MP could only wearily reply, "I'm sorry. I'm tired of talking about the FWA, and I prefer not to. All this publicity for them does nobody any good… " He could truthfully have added, "… least of all, Plaid Cymru."

Chapter Thirteen

THE GREAT CITY OF BIRMINGHAM claims with justification to be the workshop of England, and its inhabitants proudly boast that they, "Con mek anything". They cannot however make water in sufficient quantities to supply their myriad industries but must draw it from the Elan Valley reservoirs, five huge man-made lakes in the east of the bleak Cambrian mountains. The water is channelled through a series of underground pipes which connect the reservoirs with the 84 miles distant city.

During the snowy months of January and February 1967, squads of the West Wales column of the FWA reconnoitred the line of the water supply searching for a vulnerable target area. One squad took picks and shovels to test the feasibility of digging down to the actual pipe, but quickly realised the futility of that particular exercise. Another squad found an easier prospect.

Near Cefn Penarth, Crossgates, a few miles from the staid spa town of Llandrindod Wells, the Birmingham water supplies crossed a river by means of an aqueduct. At one end of the aqueduct was a manhole sealed with a padlocked lid. Once the padlock was broken off access could be gained to the interior of the aqueduct. Because of the continuous publicity given to Cayo Evans his column was under police surveillance, so it was decided that the proposed attack on the aqueduct should be carried out by one of the FWA South Wales columns. The selected column carried out its own check on the target and organised the operation.

The plan was to demolish the aqueduct completely; and by doing so cut off the main Birmingham water supply, which would have caused a severe water crisis for its 1,500,000 population almost immediately.

The evening of February 27th was very dark and a hazy ground mist blanketed most of Mid-Wales. Three FWA men set out from Swansea in an old Austin car. The driver, an Englishman, was in civilian clothes, the other two wore the insigniaed combat jackets of the FWA. Under the battered rear seat of the car was the bomb, an inflated mini car innertube with forty sticks of gelignite and a detonator strapped onto it. One of the two uniformed men, the leader, carried a shoulder-holstered Smith & Wesson 45 revolver to frighten off anyone who might try to stop them reaching their target.

The roads were nearly empty and the car made good time. What conversation that took place was terse and desultory, and kept deliberately to commonplace exchanges. The driver finally stopped the car in the shelter of some trees and the two-man assault team lifted out the bomb, then opened the boot and took from it a coil of rope and two smaller coils of wire. Slowly they picked their way across the rough terrain. It was still moonless and twice the confusing darkness caused them to miss their way, and force them to tortuously retrace their steps. Passing through one patch of woodland a frightened owl suddenly erupted past their heads, and the subordinate of the pair, his nerves tight-stretched, shouted out in wild alarm and began to crash blunderingly through the undergrowth in mindless flight. The armed man went after him, and shaking him roughly managed to calm him down.

At last they heard the sound of the river and headed directly towards it. They worked their way along the bank until the denser shadow of the long aqueduct loomed out of the darkness. Warning his nervous companion to keep a sharp ear for any sound of someone approaching, the leader went quickly to work. He broke open the manhole cover, then after fixing the ends of the separate wires to the detonator tied the rope end around the innertube and lowered it gently into the manhole. The rushing water took the floating bomb with its flow and the leader allowed the wires and rope to slip through his fingers until he felt the pre-tied knot in the rope. This signalled that the bomb was now centred in the interior of the aqueduct's mid-section. He lashed the knotted end of the rope to an adjacent tree to hold the bomb in position and completed the wiring circuit with two dry-cell torch batteries and a clock timing device, which he placed on the concrete edge of the manhole. The timer was then set to make contact at three a.m. the following morning, and the operation was completed...

But not successful. Due to a fault in the clock mechanism the bomb failed to explode. When no news of an explosion was issued by the media one of the FWA men phoned the Swansea office of the *Western Mail* to ask why they had not reported the destruction of the aqueduct. The reporter shrugged the call off as just another hoax, leaving the would-be bombers in a very invidious position. Left untouched, the bomb was reasonably safe, but if someone was to find and meddle with it, then that person could be killed. On the other hand, if they could retrieve the bomb themselves then another attempt could be made to destroy the aqueduct. Another disquieting possibility was that the police might already know of the bomb and be waiting for the bombers to make just such an attempt. But before any decision could be reached the matter resolved itself.

On the following Sunday afternoon, Tom Powell, a middle-aged sheep farmer saw the open manhole as he crossed an adjacent field and went to investigate. He was quick to notify the authorities of his find, and that same evening an army Bomb Disposal officer from Western Command, Captain, later Major Clifton Jeffries dismantled the device and detonated the unstable gelignite in a nearby wood. The resulting bang was heard for miles around, but from the FWA's point of view it was a case of the wrong time in the wrong place.

This abortive mission caused acrimonious recriminations between the various columns. It also brought the Welsh Regional Crime Squads swarming around the homes of the FWA members once more, while the police together with Birmingham Corporation officials checked and searched the entire 84 miles of pipeline, and discussed ways and means of increasing security at the vulnerable points.

An added embarrassment for the FWA was that the then Chief of Staff of the Irish Republican Army, Cathal Goulding, had agreed to send over one of his most experienced officers, Eamon O'Higgins, to establish closer liaison links with the Welsh extremist force. Instead of the hoped-for spectacular success to demonstrate the expertise of the FWA, there was this failure to be noted by the Irishman, and doubtless reported critically upon.

The Irishman had an embarrassing occurrence of his own to explain away however. When he arrived at Fishguard, Cayo Evans was waiting to greet him. Cayo was at the time being tailed by a plain-clothes policeman, and it was this officer whom the IRA man mistook for Cayo Evans. The policeman very politely pointed out the real Cayo Evans, and then followed the pair of them.

The only comfort the FWA could draw from the operation at Crossgates was that it did at least keep the FWA in the public eye, and re-affirm to the world that in Wales there were men determined to challenge the rule of England.

*   *   *

On the political front Keith Griffiths and Antony Lewis were also hard at work. They had realised that many potential recruits for nationalism were nervous of involvement in the military style actions of the FWA or the militant uniformed Patriotic Front, but could be attracted into the movement for Welsh independence by appealing to their own particular interests. To cater for these specialised tastes Griffiths and Lewis began to form a whole series of different organisations. The *Young Patriots' League* was immediately successful in enrolling a host of schoolchildren and young teenagers. This was followed by the *Llewelyn Society* whose aims as stated upon the membership cards were: *(1) To honour the memory of Llewelyn ein Llyw Olaf, the last true Prince of Wales, and to further his ideas of an independent nation free from alien domination. (2) To end the degrading insult to our nation of having the son of the English sovereign as a 'Prince of Wales'.*

The story of Prince Llewelyn possessed great romantic appeal for the extreme nationalists. In the winter of 1282 he had raised the standard of rebellion and marched an army to fight the English. The opposing forces faced each other across the Irfon bridge near Builth Wells. While separated from his army, Llewelyn was surrounded by a scouting party of English soldiers on a hillside known as Cilmeri, and killed by them. The spot where he met his death is marked by a memorial stone, erected ironically enough by an English owner of the land.

Two prominent nationalists, Harri Webb and Emrys Roberts had already done something to commemorate this symbol of Welsh resistance with their magazine, *Cilmeri Centrepoint*, but it was Tony Lewis and Keith Griffiths who now thought of staging a nationalist rally at this stone on each December 11th, the anniversary of the Prince's death. They had realised that Wales was in actual fact very poor in monuments to its patriots, the many castles being considered as monuments to the conquerors of the country.

Initially the rally was planned to be for all shades of nationalist opinion, but the first meeting was dominated by the uniformed members of the Patriotic Front and the Free Wales Army. Several Plaid Cymru people who attended waxed very indignant about this. Inevitably the rally, which took the form of a dusk torchlight march to the Cilmeri Stone, followed by speeches, Union-flag burnings and patriotic songs, was considered too violently extreme by the Plaid Cymru party, and their members were officially forbidden to attend there.

The newspapers were of course only too happy to publicise the event, which was an added irritation to the opponents of extremism. 'Mandrake' of the Sunday Telegraph wrote a dramatic account of "… hundreds of young Red Dragon Guards massing at the Cilmeri Stone…" and claimed he was the first journalist to be allowed to photograph this 'secret' rally.

Anticipating future developments the *Patriots Aid Committee* to care for the families of imprisoned nationalists was then formed. It did manage to raise a considerable sum of money in both the United Kingdom and Ireland when the FWA commandants were finally imprisoned. Unfortunately two of its members, a man from Liverpool, who always claimed to be an ex-Foreign Legionnaire, and another man from Cardiff disappeared with the funds, and were not seen again in Welsh nationalist circles.

An old source of grievance was resurrected by the formation of the *Lost Lands Liberation League*. This was an organisation to agitate for the return to Welsh sovereignty of Monmouthshire, Herefordshire and those parts of

Cheshire, Shropshire and Gloucestershire which had comprised the ancient Norman-Welsh Marches.

Even people of Royalist inclinations were catered for with the Welsh Monarchy Society. A prominent Welsh landowner, and a Plaid Cymru founder, Mr Robert Wynne was a direct relative via the line of Tudor monarchs to the Queen of England, and his family could with some justification be termed the true Welsh monarchy. Mr Wynne was very sympathetic to the Free Wales Army and when physical confrontations between police and FWA men led to the latter being arrested Robert Wynne bailed out the prisoners on many occasions. Not the normal Plaid Cymru type pacifist, he was to go on record as saying: "I'm a traditionalist. When other means fail you have to throw half a brick in somebody's face to get him to listen. The English never take anybody seriously till somebody gets killed, and they start blowing things up. Although of course this is not an advocation of violence, but it is a fact. Sad, but true!"

Yet another very thriving organisation formed by Griffiths and Lewis was the *Cofiwn Glyndwr*, the Owain Glyndŵr League. On 'Glyndŵr Day', Sept. 16th 1967, the Free Wales Army, Patriotic Front, Young Patriots' League and a militant body of Welsh Language Society supporters paraded the streets of Machynlleth, Glyndŵr's ancient capital, with drums beating and flags flying. In full uniform the jack-booted Denis Coslett with his Alsatian dog, Gelert, at his side, led the marchers. It was a direct challenge to the authorities, who had previously threatened to arrest uniformed members of these organisations. The police maintained a discreet presence, but their photographers took pictures of the marchers to add to the increasing dossier being built up by the Special Branch; and Superintendent Ernest Hickey of the Dyfed/Powys constabulary took particular notice of the leading personalities, such as Coslett,

Neil Jenkins, Owain Williams, Cayo Evans.

During the day the clenched-fist, arm-stretched Llewelyn salute was much in evidence, and tough looking FWA men seemed poised and eager to deal with any would-be disrupters of the various ceremonies. A torchlight procession was held the same night and the customary burning of the Union Jack, coupled with inflammatory speeches took place beneath the ornate clock in the centre of the town. One elderly local lady, a trifle inebriated, seized the chance to get up and make her own speech on the Town Hall steps, which was listened to with some degree of mystification by the audience.

The Cilmeri rally: "The hated flag is burned"

The Machynlleth march! Led by Denis Coslett, the extremists throw down the gauntlet of challange to the authorities

A press conference was well attended, but in the following week's newspapers the march was either played down, or equated to Neo-Nazism. A BBC television current affairs team had come to Machynlleth and Keith Griffiths angrily recalls:

"The BBC crew wanted some shots of the FWA doing manoeuvres. But they didn't go to Cayo Evans or Denis Coslett, instead they picked some fringe members, drunkards mostly in my opinion, and had a march on the mountains, and made a thorough mockery out of them. Now that went out over the air as being the FWA. It's these sort of people that I condemn, who lend themselves to that type of rubbish."

In the North Wales town of Wrexham a short, slender-bodied man with blue-grey eyes sat watching the current affairs programme with great interest. He was also a Welsh nationalist, but in contrast to the extroverts of the FWA a very quiet and retiring patriot. But this man was shortly to become one of the most fanatical and formidable of the opponents the British security services had to face in their efforts to combat the Welsh freedom movement.

His name was John Barnard Jenkins... Sergeant John Barnard Jenkins, of the British Army.

Chapter Fourteen

"**O**UR OLD MOTHER WALES is not a beautiful young girl after whom I lust, or an ugly duchess whose money and status I desire; she is old, well past her best, decrepit, boozy, and has taken strange bedfellows without the saving grace of desperation. I owe her my love and my loyalty, she is my mother. She may be a liability but is the sort of liability that a crippled child is in the eyes of its parents. If I ignore her in her hour of need no one will ever know or condemn, except myself, but I have the sort of conscience that stops functioning only at the moment I stop breathing… "

These words were written from a prison cell by a man whom Mr Justice Thompson, before passing sentence of ten years' imprisonment upon him told… "Wales will disclaim and disown such methods of promoting her interests, and those who use such methods. She will condemn the terror you continued to spread by your wicked deeds. She will expect you to be punished both for your own misdeeds and to discourage others who may be disposed to imitate you…"

The worthy judge's ire would, in the opinion of many Welsh people, have been better directed against the merciless child killers, bestial rapists and brutal thugs who infest modern life, than against a man whose only crime, again in the opinion of many Welsh people, was to love his country above himself.

But perhaps John Barnard Jenkins had sent a shiver of fear through the political Establishment of Wales, and the judge's harsh word were merely a symptom of that unease.

An unease that could be justifiably experienced, because if there was one single man in the whole of Wales who by his own intellectual and physical capabilities could have brought about a revolution, then that man would have been the prisoner who stood in the dock at the Flintshire Assizes on Monday, April 21st 1970. To John Jenkins the cause of Welsh independence was a mystical crusade as holy as any crusade blessed by Church and Monarchy...

"I took up arms because with many others I felt instinctively that the Welsh national identity, our sacred soul, our everything, was not only being threatened, but was in the last stages of survival. The military, political and economic wars have long been lost in Wales, and the final cultural annihilation has been slowly, insidiously and fatally gathering momentum.

"There are still those who believe that I was waging a physical war to achieve some sort of military victory. The strategy was military, to achieve a short term mental attitude leading to a long term political settlement. The fight was not to win a military victory, but to create a state of mind.

"Of course it can be said that violence is unnecessary, and that Plaid Cymru have the answer. To this I would agree; there is no doubt that Wales will inevitably become independent. My proviso is that by the time independence arrives the Wales we know and love/hate even now, will have long gone. The Wales we wanted, free and Welsh will be absolutely unattainable.

"At least I was prepared to sacrifice my life and freedom for my ideals. I oppose the leaders of Plaid Cymru because they are prepared to sacrifice their people, their country and their heritage, on the shrine of their respectability and pacifism... "

* * *

John Barnard Jenkins, Commander of Mudiad Amddiffyn Cymru

On the surface there can have been few more unlikely candidates for rebellion than John Jenkins. A regular non-commissioned officer in the Army Dental Corps, described by his superiors as an exemplary soldier. A happily married man with two young boys. He had everything to lose and nothing to gain by taking the course that he did. Even to himself it seems something of a mystery...

"It is generally agreed among sociologists that there is a mixture of social, environmental and genetic factors towards making the mature person. I do believe that genetics have a lot to do with it, because my approach and my attitude runs totally contrary to my upbringing. I was born of English-speaking parents in a Merthyr Tydfil area that was Anglicised more than fifty years ago. I never heard Welsh spoken until I got to school. There's no logical reason that can be accounted for environmentally why I should turn out the way I did... But I did... And as I grew older my feelings of Welshness grew stronger. My parents could not, and cannot understand it at all, they just do not understand it. I'm not even Welsh-speaking, although I've tried to learn and become fluent in the language. All the people I grew up with are equally lacking in understanding of why I'm like this... I don't understand it either...

"I think my decision to take militant action was preordained. I think people like myself are safety-valves, fail-safe mechanisms, who feel that if something is wrong, then we must do something . . . perhaps it's like a corporate consciousness, I suppose it could be said that we represent a refined sounding board. I have to believe this, there is no other explanation that would give my life up to now any logical meaning. If one accepts this theory then it gives a complete and logical meaning, if un-accepting then there is no sense to it, my life, I mean...

"I don't like blowing things up, I find it a very frightening experience. I don't like dicing with death, I don't think anyone really does, at least I haven't met anyone yet. In the army I met people who like killing things; I do not, and I do not like cruelty… But neither will I put up with certain things. Such as the things that for years had been happening against the interests of the Welsh people. When I weighed up the economic situation, the political situation and the cultural situation, particularly the latter, I took the view that the Welsh culture is our heritage. This is something we must fight to protect, and we must do this, we can't just sit there…

"It's alright for people like the harpist, Osian Ellis, who leaves Wales and then pontificates about his wonderful country and thinks that nothing is wrong with it. He forgets that the Wales which produced Welsh-speaking Welshmen like himself has now almost gone, and that the mould which produced him is not there any more. There are new types of people being produced now, who don't even know that they are Welsh. While Osian Ellis and his ilk were prepared to sit back and allow this to happen unchallenged, then I was not…"

At the time of the Clywedog bombing John Jenkins was on the fringes of the MAC organisation. But was known merely as a sympathiser, and was not actively involved. He was however a member of Plaid Cymru, and was one of the purchasers of the Clywedog Valley building plots. Even after the failure of the Party's actions at that time, he still clung to the hope that there was some constitutional way of achieving Welsh independence.

By now of course the Free Wales Army and the Patriotic Front were active, but John Jenkins had had no contacts with them. When it came, his first meeting with these two groups was a disturbing one…

"My first meeting with the FWA and the PF came about

while I was still scouting around to see if there were in Wales any constitutional groups, which through constitutional means could make the type of militant action I had in mind unnecessary. Obviously one doesn't go out to risk oneself and do damage if there is an alternative method, there is no point to it. So I was wandering around and I found myself one weekend at a Plaid Cymru Summer School. All the faithful were there, Dafydd Iwan the pop star, all the Plaid Hierarchy, and Gwynfor Evans was going to address them.

"I got there rather late and had no choice of accommodation, so ended up on the floor in a classroom where the desks had been removed and people were going to sleep on sacks etc. on the floor. Antony Lewis and Cayo Evans were in this classroom with their uniformed men, banners etc. No one knew me of course, and I had settled myself in a corner and tried to get some sleep. Cayo had by now gone out somewhere, but Lewis and his group were still there with some FWA men. I heard them whispering in a corner, and as they grew more excited the whispers became clearly audible. Suddenly I realised that they were planning to tar and feather me!

"Eventually one of them came over to me, and sat on the edge of my pallet. He began to question me. Firing the queries in rapid succession, radiating suspicion about my answers… Was I a member of Plaid Cymru? What were the aims of the party? Where had I come from? What did I think about the Trywyryn bombs?… It was quite clear that he thought I was a detective, as did everybody else who were glaring at me with undisguised hatred, and now threatening openly to tar and feather me.

"Before they could work themselves up and make a mad rush at me, I stopped my interrogator in mid-question and said, 'Look, for God's sake let me speak to whoever is in charge here.'

"It was really a very tense situation by this time. I was passed on from one to another up the chain of command, and eventually met someone from North Wales who knew me vaguely as a Plaid Cymru member. He managed to convince the rest of them that I was harmless, and from then on I was left in peace… It was ironic, the only time I was to meet the FWA and the Patriotic Front, was the occasion they wanted to tar and feather me…"

Despairing of finding any effective constitutional means of achieving what he wanted for his country, John Jenkins spent the next few months strengthening his contacts among the now almost moribund *Mudiad Amddiffyn Cymru*. It was during this period that he was to become friends with the man who was later to be tried and sentenced with him, Frederick Ernest Alders, a young part-time soldier in the Territorial Army, who earned his civilian livelihood as an aerial rigger in the Wrexham area. He was also a fanatical Welsh nationalist and patriot, but was later in an effort to save himself, to turn Queen's Evidence and betray the man he called his friend.

"I met Alders through the TA. It was all very strange, there I was, a regular soldier, yet also a member of the Territorial Army. I was stationed at Saighton Camp in Chester after returning from Germany, and lived in married quarters at Wrexham. My house was very close to the TA barracks there. I'd been playing tennis one night, and from the courts could hear a band playing. I'm a keen drummer myself, so after the game I wandered around the corner to have a look at the band. One thing led to another and before long I found myself as an instructor drummer in the TA, being paid by them as well as the Regular Army. Alders was a flautist in the band, and we drank together many times, eventually becoming close friends."

Frederick Alders, although young was a violent Welsh

nationalist. He had joined Plaid Cymru in 1965 but had shortly become convinced that the party was a waste of time, and that political militancy and explosions like Tryweryn would be needed to achieve independence for Wales. It was not long before he became a willing and eager aide of John Jenkins. A great deal of reorganising and re-shuffling had been taking place in the Mudiad Amddiffyn Cymru and eventually it was decided that John Jenkins, by now a trusted member of the organisation, should prove himself by carrying out an operation. The target chosen was the water pipeline between Lake Fyrnwy and Liverpool. Lake Fyrnwy, a favourite beauty spot for tourists, is surrounded by the wooded slopes of the Berwyn mountains in Montgomeryshire. Four massive 48 inch pipes run from it to the city of Liverpool, 60 miles to the North-East. Most of their way they lie underground but on the Denbighshire/ Montgomeryshire border, some 400 yards from the centre of the village of Llanrhaeadr-ym-Mochnant, the four pipes emerge to stretch over the narrow River Rhaeadr. The target was a popular choice, the bitterness over Liverpool's handling of the Tryweryn issue being still deeply felt by the Welsh nationalists. John Jenkins wasted no time…

"I had already scouted out the land around the village on several occasions, and knew exactly where and what everything was. There were four pipes down there and they emerged from underground in only one place, which was over a stream in the middle of afield a few hundred yards from the village proper. Now if we had got the four pipes, which we could easily have done, it would have meant the water would have risen so rapidly that the village would have in all probability been swept away. So we decided to do just the one pipe. It might also crack the adjoining pipe, but that would present no danger to the village. We didn't want the villagers to suffer in any way since it was through no fault of theirs that the pipes ran by them.

"A week prior to the night of the operation I went to the south, and from one of my contacts there got 14½1bs of gelignite, because at that time I carried no stores. The geli was extremely leaky, so leaky in fact that we practically had to carry it in a bucket. I fixed the bomb up, and put in two detonators. I used two because it's surprising how many dud detonators there are. Half our bombs failed to go off because of dud detonators. There is no way of telling how old a detonator is, and no way of testing it without using it, which makes it rather difficult. We used the Venner clock as a timing device because it was very reliable. But unfortunately this was one of the very old types which worked on a spring system. The more modern ones work like a ratchet, you set them and the two contact points move slowly together like the jaws of pincers. The old type worked so that when the spring was released it would jump open and touch the opposing contact point. The one I had was very old, and as it happened very dangerous too, very shaky mechanism, and of course anything with a spring tends to be more erratic than the ratchet system.

"On the night of the operation, September 30th 1967, I got myself an alibi. The way the TA is run it is really only a boozing club. Once a week put on your uniform and go down for a booze-up. It's fair to say this was the case at Wrexham. So I went up to the sergeants' mess at Wrexham and started drinking, standing quietly by myself, but letting people know I was there, then slipped out halfway through the evening. It was misty and wet. I had driven to the barracks in my car and left it in the barrack courtyard. My friend Alders was waiting inside the car for me and we went straight on down to the village. We reached the area fairly early so it was necessary to wait until it became darker. The place we had previously chosen to wait in was at a noted beauty spot, a waterfall close to Mochnant. The fact that there were people in cars around that spot wouldn't create any attention because many trippers visited it.

"Once it was dark we went to the pipes. I carried the explosives and Alders brought the timing device etc. Since the explosives were very unstable I sent Alders away while I placed them, it was a dodgy business, then set the timer for two o'clock in the morning. We then went back home. I went directly to my house, took off the overalls I'd slipped on over my uniform, burned them and went back to the sergeants' mess. I'd been away about two hours and the beer I'd left in my glass had gone a bit flat, but it tasted good. The blokes in the mess wouldn't have noticed if I'd been away for a week because they were all half-drunk and I'd been with no one in particular. The general effect, because I then stayed there drinking until quite late, was that I'd been there all night with the rest.

"The first news about the explosion and destruction of the pipe came through next day at twelve o'clock on the radio. My feelings about the matter were very very mixed. Up until then I had never been actively involved, that is I'd never done any jobs. People have since said to me that when I was actually doing the job it must have been exhilarating, thrilling etc. It's not really. I didn't find it thrilling at all. It was a wet night, our clothes were wet and soaking, it was dark and I couldn't see anything. I couldn't be sure that the Special Branch weren't watching. I'd kept an eye on the target of course, I knew that there were no guards coming around to check it, but still there were the doubts.

"My basic feeling going home in the car that night was one of great sadness because it had come to this. The thing is that the first time you deliberately break the law, and for Alders and myself it was the first time, then that is the first time you snatch the blinkers away. The web that has been carefully and steadily drawn about you since the day you were born is suddenly cut through. All the taboos, such as the policeman is a nice chap, and the government is always right, and the state is there for the citizen's own good, all these things had grown and grown on me all my life, and I wasn't a youngster, I was in the army and in my mid-thirties. So basically I was reacting violently against everything that up until then had been the whole basis of my existence. What I felt when I left that bomb on the pipeline was that since before my action I had been within the law and a respected member of the public within the law; now I was outside the law… and I was filled with a sort of sadness, a sense of loss because I had cut myself off. I felt a totally different person. Once one has taken a bite against the state and it succeeds, then one is totally different, totally divorced. I felt that I could then for the first time look at things with complete objectivity, because I no longer had these 'should I or shouldn't I' doubts. I could go against the state, I had gone against the state, and I was still here… "

* * *

The Llanrhaeadr bomb hit the headlines. *The Dam Busters strike again, Police step up hunt for saboteurs. FWA questioned on Pipe blast. Blast village fear a killing next time.*

It was announced that a special guard would patrol the bomb site for the next three weeks. The villagers of Llanrhaeadr could be forgiven for considering this action as a case of closing the stable door after the horse had bolted. The Secretary of State for Wales, Mr Cledwyn Hughes, said, "The explosion would be deeply resented and deplored by the people of Wales. I have been gravely disturbed to learn that explosives were used to damage the pipelines supplying water," and he theorised: "This would appear to be an act of sabotage by extremists."

There was an immediate dispute as to who should pay for the damage, estimated cost £10,000. Mr Cyril Carr, leader of Liverpool Corporation's Liberals, urged that the government should supply the repair funds. One potential source of revenue was not taken advantage of. That was to charge admission fees to the scores of sight-seers who crowded into the village over the next few weeks.

Neil Jenkins, school teacher and treasurer of the Welsh Language Society hailed the explosion as another act of defiance against English government and wished that all four pipes had been blown up.

The reaction of the villagers of Llanrhaeadr, some five households having lost their windows in the blast, seemed curiously ambivalent. "We sympathise with the bombers' ideals, but not with violence," the local garage proprietor told reporters.

The Plaid Cymru leaders were livid. Mr Humphrey Roberts, former chairman of the Caernarfon branch, offered £100 reward for the capture of the bombers. A Montgomeryshire member suspected that Irish friends of the FWA were responsible, and gave his reasons. "Members of the FWA have friends in Dublin and last year's explosion at Clywedog almost coincided with sabotage in Dublin (the blowing up of Nelson's Column). These men have worked together in the past and I would not be surprised to learn that the actual saboteurs came from Eire via Holyhead. After all the IRA have a lot more experience of this sort of thing than the FWA."

The fiery Mr E.G. Millward was more explicit. "The whole thing stinks!" A little later he again turned on his *bête noir*, the Free Wales Army, calling them, "These irresponsible political jokers." He went on to say: "The question needs to be asked, 'Is the political establishment allowing these nonentities to exist in the hope that they will do maximum damage to Plaid Cymru?' They wear paramilitary uniforms, which in itself is an offence. They advocate force, armed insurrection — against whom it is not clear. Yet the authorities leave them quietly alone, and their most ludicrous comments regularly hit the headlines in the 'Yellow Press'! These men are effete nonentities, but like so many nonentities could be extremely dangerous." Mr Millward called on the police to get tough with the FWA. This last demand seemed to at least one of his listeners to be a self-contradiction. Surely the police were acting correctly in ignoring effete nonentities and paper tigers; after all, what damage could such people conceivably do?

Cayo Evans immediately claimed the bomb as the work of the Northern Brigade of the Free Wales Army, but said he had no idea as to the identities of the individuals responsible. He then figuratively sat back and awaited the onslaught of the press. It was not long in coming. Antony Currah of the widely circulated *Sun* newspaper came to seek interviews with Cayo, his lieutenant Vernon Griffiths, and the South Wales commandant, Denis Coslett. The journalist was looking for sensationalism, and the three men were happy to oblige him. *We're ready for War*, the headline screamed; *FWA say they have guns hidden in the hills*. The interviewees claimed that the army strength, open and hidden, totalled 7,000 men; and that a council of seven wealthy and influential Welsh people controlled the FWA. In one solo interview Denis Coslett warned that all water supplies from Wales to England would be crippled within six months if a fair price for that commodity was not paid to the Welsh. Antony Currah was later asked his personal opinion of the Commandants, and he replied, "I believe they were fanatics and that they believed every word they said."

In the midst of all the uproar and excitement the police

appeared to be the only cool heads. While the Mid-Wales force checked the site for forensic evidence and questioned known extremists, the number Eight Regional Crime Squad, under the direction of Mr John Parkman ranking as an Assistant Chief Constable, went on painstakingly building up a sophisticated intelligence network to try and trace the bombers. A spokesman said at Newtown Police HQ where the hunt for the saboteurs was based, "It is obvious that all these incidents are the work of a small band of extremists. At this stage we cannot tell whether they are trained experts in explosives, or merely amateurs with very good luck."

During the coming months the bombs were to increase in frequency and the police were soon in no doubt that those responsible were both very expert, and very lucky…

Chapter Fifteen

EVER SINCE THE FIRST SHAFT of the first coalmine was sunk the people of the mining villages of South Wales have paid with blood and suffering for every ton of coal brought to the surface. The list of pit disasters is a long and terrible scroll. At 9.15 a.m. on the morning of the 21st October 1966, the small village of Aberfan added its name to that scroll. Only this time it was not the miners below the ground who paid the price of coal, but children…

The huge Number Seven waste tip of the Merthyr Vale Colliery roared down in a black avalanche of water and slurry, and 144 children, men and women died.

The fact that the majority of the tip avalanche victims were young Junior School children moved the hearts, and perhaps the consciences of the world, and from more than forty countries donations flooded into a Disaster Fund, set up to help financially those who had suffered grievous loss. The Fund was officially closed in January 1967, but money still poured in until the total reached was more than one and three quarters million pounds sterling.

A provisional committee was set up on the 2nd November 1966 to deal with any immediate applications for assistance, and a sub-committee was formed to draw up a draft Trust Deed for the Fund. The business of making application to the Committee for relief, and that application being investigated, smacked too much of the bitterly-remembered Means Test, and was deeply resented by the proud people of Aberfan. It should be noted that although this money had

Carnage at Aberfan

been freely given by people deeply moved by Aberfan's grief, bureaucracy considered that the villagers of Aberfan were not capable of administering the fund, or of deciding what to do with the money. The first Committee did not include a single representative from Aberfan.

A Parents and Residents Association was then formed in the village and, backed by their solicitors, pressured for representation on the Fund Committee. When the Trust Deed for the fund was signed in January 1967, the bureaucrats had reluctantly decided to allow five Aberfan representatives elected by the villagers to sit on the Committee of fifteen members.

As time went by salaried officials, not from Aberfan, were employed by the Fund Committee, drawing very substantial remuneration. The offices of the Fund were established in Merthyr Tydfil and it quickly became apparent that the majority of the Fund Committee sitting in Merthyr identified themselves with authority and the seat of local government. A lot of tension was engendered, and many of the original donors felt strongly that the Fund should be disbursed to the bereaved families. That was whom the money had been sent for, not to pay salaries and expenses to officials and bureaucrats. The donors failed to understand why this disbursement had not been carried out immediately. Was the Fund to be frozen in the Treasury, as the funds established following the pit disaster at Senghenydd in 1913 and Gresford in 1934 had been? The major part of both of those relief funds are being still held by the Treasury to this day.

The months dragged on and still nothing was done about distributing the money, and the bereaved families had received nothing, although the salaried officials drew their pay. Every appeal to the Fund administrators was met with the excuse that since it was a Trust Fund the law could not allow such a distribution. John Summers, an author and journalist had gone to Aberfan during the terrible days following the disaster. He had come to know and share the grief of the afflicted families. Members of the Parents and Residents Association came to him seeking help and advice, unable themselves to penetrate the bland walls of officialdom. John Summers realised that drastic and unorthodox measures were the only way to ruffle bureaucratic complacency. What was needed was some organisation prepared to challenge authority. Previously the author had formed a relationship with the rebel Free Wales Army commandants, and it was to these men that he and the desperate villagers of Aberfan turned. At their invitation

Denis Coslett, David Bonar Thomas and another FWA man came to meet representatives of the Parents Association in September 1967. They met at the Aberfan Hotel and the FWA men upon hearing the story of official procrastination were immediately eager to help.

The following day more than fifty FWA men with banners, drums and uniforms assembled at Merthyr and marched through the town. Denis Coslett called a press conference at the Morlais Arms and several reporters were present, including John Christopher of the *Daily Express*. Flanked by his fellow commandants, Denis Coslett asked the journalists to publish the following ultimatum:

"If a sum of £5,000 was not paid within a week to each of the bereaved families of Aberfan then the Active Service Units of the Free Wales Army would take immediate action. The Merthyr Tydfil Town Hall, the Committee Rooms of the Fund, plus the offices of the solicitor being paid to act as Secretary/Treasurer of the Fund would all be blown up. If, after this, nothing was still done, then the County Government Offices would be blasted, and following that the Government Offices in Cardiff would be destroyed… "

Whether it was the intervention of the FWA which persuaded officialdom will probably never be known. But during the following Friday it was announced that the sum of £5,000 would be paid immediately to each of the bereaved families. It seemed that laws could be broken after all.

The gratitude of the people of Aberfan towards the FWA and John Summers was tangibly expressed when engraved watches were presented to the author and to Denis Coslett in recognition of their help by the Parents Association. Fred Grey, a leading member of the Association who had himself lost a child in the disaster, went on record as saying: "If it wasn't for the FWA the families would never have received a penny."

Even today, 1979, it is possible to hear the same feelings of gratitude to the FWA expressed in Aberfan: "The lads of the FWA, and John Summers did a good job for us. When no one else would help us, they did. There was no one else we could turn to until they came along. Great to us they were. Great lads… !" — A bereaved parent of Aberfan, April 30th 1979.

The last word on this can well be left to Denis Coslett.

"I think one of my proudest moments in life, was to see those people at Aberfan having that bit of cash. It wasn't the money for itself they wanted. Their grief couldn't be soothed by money. It was just the recognition that it was their children who had paid the price — and no one else!"

Chapter Sixteen

Behold the Red Dragon Flag
Is floating across the silver sea,
And the soul of Wales is crying
In the very heart of me.

Crying Justice, Crying Vengeance
Pray my sons for strength anew,
For the many who'll be dying
At the falling of the dew...

The new Battle Hymn of the Welsh Republic was sung by the soldiers of the Free Wales Army wherever they gathered, and it seemed that the flame of nationalism was well and truly alight throughout the Principality. A former High Sheriff of Cardiganshire, Major W.H. Rhydian Llewelyn was reputed to have stated that the problem of Welsh rural de-population could be rectified by bringing in Pakistani settlers. Cymdeithas yr Iaith immediately reacted to this by smashing all the windows at his home near Pontrhydfendigaid, and police guards had to be mounted to prevent further serious damage being done. A proposal to build a new town in Mid-Wales for the relief of English overspill was met with the threat to blow up any buildings in the course of construction. Brawls were frequent between young hotheads of the nationalist movement and visiting Englishmen who spoke slightingly of Wales.

Meetings took place between officers of the Scottish Liberation Army and the Free Wales Army high command. At these meetings the formation of an amalgamated Celtic

Army was discussed, and aid was promised to the Welshmen; which actually did materialise in the shape of a consignment of sawn-off shotguns given to the Llanelli column of the FWA by their Scottish allies. Cayo Evans was also granted a commission as Honorary Captain of the Scottish Liberation Army.

John Tyndal's National Front contacted the FWA, wanting to know their political aims. Men claiming to represent the. Jewish Board of Deputies contacted the Patriotic Front with similar motives, and were gratified to learn that the PF were great admirers of Israel. Very friendly relationships were established with the Brittany Liberation Front, which was itself involved in a bombing campaign in France. There have traditionally been close links between Celtic Wales and Celtic Brittany, both their native tongues are Cymric Gaelic, their national anthems are the same *Hen Wlad Fy Nhadau* (Land of My Fathers); and they both possess sizeable minorities of extreme nationalists who believe their land should be free of foreign domination. Yann Goulet, the chief of the FLB (Brittany Liberation Front) was an exile in Eire with many of his friends, and they issued a newsletter in both English and Breton published in Ireland. In most editions of the newsletter space was given to Welsh nationalist writers, a courtesy also extended by the IRA's *United Irishman*, and the Scottish nationalists' *Sqian Dubh* newsletter edited by Major F.A.C. Boothby.

An alliance of Welsh and Breton was projected which would entail networks of safe houses to be used by each other's men on the run, and even exchanges of specialists to carry out operations on behalf of each other's organisation. A similar alliance was talked about between representatives of the IRA and FWA but never really came to anything — possibly because at this time the internal dissension later to lead to the splitting of the IRA into Provos and Officials was already ongoing. Some consignments of weapons and ammunition were later to be supplied to the Welshmen by the IRA, and particularly good and close relationships were developed between the South Walian columns and certain IRA cells. Welshmen going to Ireland helped their friends among the IRA in various ways.

Other more exotic revolutionary groups made fleeting appearances at the mansion home of Cayo Evans. Croats, Basques, Flemish, Manx, Quebecois and Palestine Liberation Organisation members knocked at the door, spent a while inside, and went away mostly never to return. One idea which constantly re-occurred was that of forming an 'International Celtic Guard'. It was the concept of two very colourful characters, Eamon O'Higgins, the IRA liaison officer, and an Irish doctor living in the English Midlands, Dr John Brookes, who according to his own account had served with the British Army for eleven years and was at Dunkirk. For half his service he was an other-ranker, digging trenches etc. but then qualified as a doctor, finishing his service as a captain in the RAMC. Apparently he was a medical student in the Irish Free State prior to the war, but got into trouble with the Irish authorities for throwing Republican pamphlets from the top of the Dublin Nelson's Column. When it was discovered by the British Army during the war that Brookes was a one-time medical student, they enabled him to finish his studies and qualify. The doctor, a big powerful man and a strong Celtic nationalist, gave his sympathies to most freedom movements, including the Nagas of India. The 'Ancient Order of Irish Chieftains' founded by Brookes was to be the putative parent of the 'Celtic Guard'. This order prints a newspaper and also marches in parades at various places. Denis Coslett met the doctor through the St. Patrick's Day parade in Birmingham when some 20,000 people march through the streets and all the counties of Ireland are represented. Denis Coslett marched at Birmingham with an FWA contingent, and Brookes was directly behind them carrying his own huge self-designed banner.

The Celtic Guard never became fully operational, but it did attract to it a number of adherents in various Celtic countries, and among other things issued the 'Celtic Cross' for valour in the field to members of the various freedom movements. Coslett himself was later to receive this award, as were the Bretons who carried out the attack on the police station at St. Brieuc in France in September 1968.

Some years later at the time of the great Washington peace protests against the war in Vietnam a curious reminder of that International Celtic Army was headlined in the British press as *Guerrilla Army plot foiled*: One journalist, Arthur Tietjen wrote a detailed account:

"Special Branch detectives have foiled a plot to unite and arm Welsh, Scottish, and Irish extremists. Nine arrests have been made in London and other parts of the country. Security men were tipped off 18 months ago that nationalists were completing plans to join forces to win independence for Wales, Scotland and Ulster. The initiative seems to have come from Welsh extremists. They believed they could whip up nationalist fervour in Prince Charles' investiture year. They were joined eagerly by the IRA which saw an opportunity to stockpile arms. Scotland Yard uncovered a plan to create cells of armed insurrectionists in London, Scotland, Wales, the Midlands and the North. A series of raids was made in different areas resulting in the recovery of stolen arms and ammunition.

"In London, Special Branch raided a house in Hackney and found documents outlining the main plan. A diary contained the names and addresses of sympathisers from all three extremist groups, including several Roman Catholic priests.

"In Essex they infiltrated a group of five young Irishmen plotting to steal Sterling sub-machineguns and ammunition. Two of the group were caught and are now serving seven years.

"In the north a swoop was made on a separate group suspected of attempting to obtain firearms.

"In the Midlands Special Branch officers based on Birmingham recovered Lee-Enfield rifles, — 38 revolvers and ammunitions.

"In Scotland detectives discovered that nationalists had offered support to extremists from Wales and Eire. They kept watch on a group headed by a Glasgow woman.

"It was in Wales that the nationalist groups held their action conference. Known leaders from all three countries, including the woman from Glasgow, met in Prestatyn to discuss the link up. Members of the Irish squad of the Special Branch were drafted into Wales to keep track on the movements of IRA men filtering into the country on the ferries at Fishguard, Swansea and Liverpool. The first object of the plotters was to steal arms and ammunition from factories in England. They have had some success. Captured snipers' guns used by the Ulster rioters were made in Britain…"

*   *   *

But all this was to happen later, not in 1967. In that year although many revolutionary movements were eager to help the Welsh extremists, governments were more reluctant, as Tony Lewis related…

"We went, two of us, up to the United Arab Republic embassy in London wearing full uniform; I believe Nasser was then in power. They were very sympathetic and we met the Ambassador. Unfortunately the Embassy was in the process of being closed and they couldn't do anything for us at that time, but were very insistent that we contact them at some later date. The Arabs asked us many questions, and I think that if the time had been more favourable they would have given us help with money and arms.

"We also went to the Cuban embassy. The Ambassador was then a woman, and couldn't or wouldn't see us, so we met the First Secretary instead. A very supercilious, old-school-tie type, who was totally unlike our conception of a Castro revolutionary. Needless to say we found no aid or comfort there."

The only real practical help was to come from that cradle of rebels, Ireland. Vivian Davies, a stocky man with bright red hair whose round tough face bore the marks of his amateur boxing experience was the commandant of a Swansea column. During his time with the FWA he had many exchanges with the IRA. Vivian Davies was also a good illustration of the very wide social strata the FWA were drawn from:

"When I was a kid we lived in Forest Fach at Swansea. It was a rough upbringing, a broken home and violent father. We had no electric light, at times no food or even shoes. But my upbringing has nothing to do with my nationalism, although you'd get a lot of these head-shrinkers put it down to that. Because of the broken home and disruption and what have you, but it had nothing to do with how I feel about my country.

"I didn't like Welsh lessons at school, so I can't say that I was a nationalist then… As a child you don't understand things. The old saying is that the older you get the wiser, and the older and wiser I got, the stronger I became towards patriotism. I see it as a duty to be patriotic. It's more of an emotional thing with me, than an economic or financial thing. I think Denis (Denis Coslett) introduced me to Welsh nationalism, and Cayo of course.

"I was introduced to Denis through another friend who'd worked in the mines with him. When I met Denis he was already a Welsh Nat and he spoke about this and that and I saw then, straight away, that it was my duty to be the same as him. After that first meeting I only saw Coslett about three times in six months. During that time he joined the FWA, and when I met him again I joined up myself and began to form my own column. I thought the FWA was great, and I was very proud to wear its uniform. The English have been the oppressing nation throughout the world for five hundred years. I would have done anything to get from under their iron fist.

"I was never one for going into pubs to recruit or to work at FWA business. I know how closely the police act in concert with a lot of licensees. Too many licensees stand behind their bars ostensibly taking no notice, but in fact absorbing everything that's said, which they then pass on to their police cronies. There was pretty strong support for the FWA around Swansea, but being a cosmopolitan city they didn't all think of nationalism as I do. I had a bit of trouble at first recruiting activists. I had supporters, but not members, they wanted to see the outcome first. Eventually I had a few members who used to participate in capers. Some of my men used to get explosives for me from where they worked in the mines, but at that time I had no idea of how to construct bombs. The stuff I was given was stockpiled.

"I didn't used to drill my blokes like Coslett drilled his, you know marching up and down and all that stuff. I should think that eventually there were at least four columns in Swansea, but there was a bit of overlapping with Llanelli, which was always a very strong FWA town. For me, the ideal column would be about six or seven men, three active, the rest sleepers.

Vivian Davies on field maneouvers

"My personal group numbered around half a dozen, I didn't want any more. I used to walk around in uniform, I never had any trouble from strangers because of that. You see there may not have been hundreds of actual members of the FWA in Swansea, but there were literally thousands of sympathisers.

We used to train in the mountains, doing firing exercises

etc. I remember one big exercise we held at the Roman-made lake above Llanddewi Brefi called Llyn-y-gwaith. There were something like sixty to seventy men there. The exercise was a mock battle between the Northern and Southern columns. We always used live ammunition, and I managed to get up into the trees and throw a bandolier of ammo onto the Northerners' cooking fire. All hell broke loose, I've never seen men take cover so quickly in my life.

"As regards myself, in fairness to the Swansea police, I had no hassle because of the FWA membership from them, not like the hassle a great many of our lads were subjected to when the situation hotted up. The local police looked upon me as the village idiot. They thought I was an Audie Murphy-type crank. They had no inkling at all as to what was going to be the outcome of all this military-style nonsense, which is what it appeared to them at the beginning. But it shows what they thought of us in the end regarding cranks and village idiots. They spent thousands, no millions, protecting their interests and putting on a show trial.

"My column did a lot with the IRA; we had a lot of support, arms, explosives, the know-how on guerrilla and terrorist tactics. The arms were mainly old Thompsons etc. The boxes would come on a Dutch coaster to Swansea docks, and we would get it from them on the docks. The boxes were lucky dips really, could be anything in them. Half a dozen deliveries came over a period of time. The Swansea CID never caught on to what was happening. They used to laugh and joke about us, and about me in my uniform, but even when the bombs were going off they never seemed to connect that and our lads. At the time I knew a lot of the police personally, there were one or two sympathisers among them, which all helped.

"Periodically some of our boys would go over to

Southern Ireland to shift stuff around for the IRA. They would use cars with GB registration and act like tourists. They would shift arms from one cache to another, and act as couriers. I was pretty close with some of the Irish, I went over myself on a couple of occasions. In County Cork they hold a Welsh Week every year. A group of Welsh people go over to Ireland and are entertained, and later some Irish come over here for the same purpose. I went to Cork in full uniform, taking it in my suitcase and as soon as we arrived putting it on. We'd go into pubs for a drink and the locals would look you up and down for a couple of hours, and then approach and ask what part you were from, who you were, and what was the uniform? And while talking they'd keep their eyes on the uniform, up and down, up and down.

"While we were in Cork we seemed to be unable to hire a car at any of the car hire places, although other Welsh people were having no trouble like that. We couldn't understand this, until finally at one place the mechanic told my friends, 'You've got no chance, boys, not while you've got that IRA bloke in uniform with you. He'll take it over the border and we'll get it blown to bits… ' "

Chapter Seventeen

IT HAD BEEN widely known for several years that Prince Charles was to be formally invested as the Prince of Wales in Caernarfon on July 1st 1969. Although in 1967 this forthcoming event was comfortably remote yet it was well-entrenched in the forefront of both nationalist and Establishment consciousness. The extremist groups saw the future ceremony as an affront to the Welsh nation, and as an abhorrent imposition of an alien regime. It was decided by the Patriotic Front and the FWA that they would begin a campaign directed against the Investiture, to try and prevent it taking place and to use this anti-campaign to attract further world-wide attention and publicity for their cause.

An umbrella organisation, the *Anti Investiture Front* was set up by the ubiquitous organisers, Griffiths and Lewis, to cover this fresh campaign in mid-1967. Through the media of the press, including the American *New York Times*, Italian, Australian and German magazines, the Anti-Investiture Front quickly gave notice of its intentions. The potential threat of harm coming to Prince Charles and other members of the Royal Family was sufficient for John Parkman, the Regional Crime Squad director to be called to secret talks in late 1967 at Buckingham Palace, the Home Office and the Welsh Office. There was also a noticeable alteration in the relationship be tween the police and the extreme nationalists. Harassment began, surveillance was increased, and open hostility replaced what had been a reasonably amicable confrontation between the opposing sides.

Frost meets the Welsh rebels

The ever-acute David Frost was quick to secure the now more than ever newsworthy FWA and Patriotic Front for an appearance on his programme at Rediffusion's Wembley Park studios on October 20th 1967, the anniversary of the battle of El Alamein. Against the backdrop of his sycophantic showbiz environment the noted satirical fancies of David Frost were displayed to their full extent as his friend, actor Lance Percival did a commercial impersonation of Field Marshal Montgomery, another actor reminisced on how he had grown geraniums on the bridge of a warship, a New Orleans jazz band blared, and Vera Lynn sang *Lili Marlene* yet again. Frost referred to Denis Coslett, who wore an eyepatch because of an infection of his damaged eye-socket, as Dai Dayan the Welsh version of the Israeli soldier, and was generally facetious about the FWA and its aims. It would have been interesting to see if the satirist would have been equally flippant had he conducted his interview on an isolated Welsh mountainside far from tame audiences and the bright lights of London.

Parallel to the Anti-Investiture Front, the secret MAC group were also formulating a basic long-term strategy to centre on the Investiture. Simply they intended that every time a member of the Royal Family, or others, stepped foot in Wales to discuss the Investiture there would be an explosion. The central policy was aimed against the Investiture. The pipeline attacks were to be of dual intent: a) to protest against the exploitation of water, b) to show the group's muscles and capability. The reasoning was that the thinking of the authorities would be: "Here are these things happening and there is danger involved for the Prince. We must clamp down hard in Wales… "

John Jenkins was now a man of influence in the MAC, and he was able to postulate his own theories. "There are certain basic pre-requisites to a successful revolution. Among them economic disturbance, lack of stability, disenchantment with bureaucracy. But on top of that, which comes back to my basic view of society, is this: 99% of society is the man in the street, and he is indifferent. If something doesn't affect him directly he doesn't want to know. He may express some concern over Northern Ireland etc. but basically he doesn't want to be involved. There is nothing he needs to do about these problems; he doesn't lose self-esteem by not involving himself.

"Half of society's remaining one percent are the agencies of the state, they have the whole power of the state machineries behind them, and they can bring the whole mighty power of the mass media to bear on whatever object they choose to. The other half percent of society are people like myself. What we are fighting about basically is the question of the control of the minds of the masses. I could not hope to match the publicity machine of the rulers. I think our Establishment has the most magnificent propaganda machine the world has ever seen, but I don't blame them for this as such. This state is a state the same as all others, and it has the same objectives as all others. A state is based on necessity and expediency, not morality. Certain things must be done to maintain the status quo. If they can be done in such a way as to please the public, then good. If they can't, then do them quietly and push them under the carpet.

"In Wales we could not call upon that most constant of revolutionary aims, the foreign power whose mass media is at the rebels' disposal, like the Irish can call upon the Americans, or the Cypriots call upon the Greeks, and obtain as a bonus technical aid and assistance. We had none of these things. Our base was here in Wales. We couldn't, for example, call upon 12 million Welsh-Americans and they'd be up in arms. They wouldn't, they assimilate too easily, their bread is too well buttered... So the only way we could get personally to the mass of Welsh people was to involve them in conflict. The only way to involve them in conflict is to have a soldier beating their door down with a rifle butt, and the only way you'll get that, is by carefully planned violence... That is, you initiate something that will bring retribution, and the retribution will fall indiscriminately. It happened in Cyprus where from a friendly village there would come a shot as the troops were passing. No one knows who pulled the trigger, so the whole village is searched and perhaps manhandled. In 24 hours that once friendly village is full of enemies. You see the psychology of people is to hate the end result, not what initially caused it. Therefore the average man's anger will not be directed against the rebel who blew up the bridge, or shot the Lord Mayor, it will be directed against the soldier who batters down his door and rips up his floorboards, for he is an innocent man and has done nothing wrong... That is the classic pattern for raising an apathetic population, and gradually it could have come about like that here in Wales.

"Take the year prior to the Investiture, it brought many middle-class Welshmen into a type of front line. Following the bombs and other incidents he suddenly found himself being watched by Special Branch men, seeing them at meetings, having them question and follow him. There was the case of the little village up in the Llŷn Peninsula where the local school was being closed down. A meeting was held to discuss this and there in the audience were two strangers, later admitted by the local police to have been Special Branch. Imagine the reaction of the local worthies — 'What the hell is this? We're law-abiding, respectable people; this is like *1984*.'

"The people of that area were immediately alienated by the presence of the Special Branch. This was happening all over Wales, and straight away you have the nice ripe ground in which the rebel can flourish. To create a revolution it is only necessary to raise the temperature a few degrees to overcome people's innate apathy. Because the authorities will always over-react, they always do and always have; and what the Minister in Whitehall directs, and what the policeman and soldier in the firing line does, are very different things. There is a gap between what the minister knows is required, and what the soldier or policeman thinks is necessary; and in that gap lies the rebel's salvation… "

* * *

The first opportunity to strike directly against the Investiture came very quickly. The Temple of Peace and Health in Cardiff Civic Centre, Cathays Park, only two hundred yards from the Welsh Police Headquarters was to be the venue for an all-Wales conference of Lord Mayors, Borough Heads, Lord Lieutenants etc. to discuss plans for Prince Charles' Investiture. The conference was to take place on November 17th 1967, and accompanied by the Secretary of State for Wales, Cledwyn Hughes, the Earl of Snowdon, then Princess Margaret's husband and as Constable of Caernarfon Castle jointly responsible with the Duke of Norfolk for organising the future ceremony, was to address the five hundred delegates.

A cell of the MAC organisation was based in Cardiff, and they wasted no time after hearing of the conference in deciding to create an incident which would leave no doubt as to their determination to prevent any member of the Royal Family being allowed trouble-free access to Wales.

Carrying a canvas holdall between them, two of the cell members walked casually along the King Edward VII Avenue towards the massive bronze doors at the front of the Temple of Peace. The time was 10.30 p.m. on the night of the 16th November. A quick glance around to check all was clear, then the bag-carrier was given a leg-up by his companion, and the holdall containing the 15lbs bomb was pushed to the rear of the lintel above the huge bronze doors. Equally casually the two men sauntered away from the building, and the bomb set to explode at 4 a.m. the following morning ticked the hours away.

At exactly 4.04 a.m. the explosive blasted into ruin the front rooms of the Temple, tearing the heavy metal panels from the doors, smashing glass, masonry, furniture. Estimated damage, £20,000. As if this were not enough irritation for the police, the Welsh Language Society had also planned a demonstration to meet Lord Snowdon and the Secretary of State, so when they arrived at 11.30 a.m. the two dignitaries were confronted with a wrecked conference hall and a large hostile crowd of banner-waving, jeering demonstrators. The police, justifiably incensed, waded into the crowd and fighting took place which resulted in 13 arrests. Tony Lewis was among those arrested…

"The day of the demonstration happened to coincide with an interview I was due to have at the Cardiff College of Music concerning a teaching post (Lewis is a highly gifted musician). Since the demonstration was staged by the Patriotic Front, as well as the Language Society, I couldn't very well not show up at it. So I went along dressed up in my best suit, and carrying my briefcase. I was arrested for obstructing Lord Snowdon's car for ten seconds. Gethin (Keith Griffiths) and some other lads were shoved into the Black Maria with me. Gethin had eggs in his pocket which he had intended to throw, and the police smashed the eggs. Gethin retaliated by smearing the resulting mess over the inside of the van's windows and sticking his anti-investiture poster across them. The Maria broke down in the middle of the crowd and there was this farcical situation of posters going up and being ripped down from the windows.

"At the police station the lads began to sing rebel songs, and from the end cell a drunk asked me, 'What's up mate? Have they arrested a bloody choir?'

"After a few hours a helpful policeman phoned the College of Music and told them that Antony Lewis had been arrested so could not attend there that day. Unfortunately I have a namesake there, a senior lecturer, and the college thought it was he, since that day he was away from home on a trip and couldn't be contacted. It took quite a lot of explaining when I was eventually able to attend for interview… "

The police had reacted swiftly after the explosion had occurred, setting up road-blocks and raiding the homes of known extremists, but despite Head of Cardiff's CID, Detective Chief-Supt. David Morris' optimism of apprehending the bombers, and Cledwyn Hughes' confident promise of early arrests, no one was ever convicted of this offence. Among the politicians it was once more an example of the cat among the pigeons. Gwynfor Evans MP, president of Plaid Cymru claimed that the bomb was a deliberate attempt to discredit the official nationalist party, and that together with the preceding bombs it was the work of Government secret agents. This accusation naturally evoked angry rebuttals from the Government. The newspapers gave the bombing a lot of space, many claiming that the Welsh people were 'Up in arms and outraged' by the occurrence. A fund for the repair of the Temple was opened but in six months it had totalled only £800 donated mainly from industry. Outrage didn't extend to giving large amounts of money it seemed. A further aggravation to the police was that the bombing triggered a rash of hoax bomb calls, which although the work of fools meant many hours of extra work for men already stretched to their limits by the serious extremists.

It was now clear to the Heads of Britain's security services that a real, and potentially lethal threat to public order existed in Wales. It was decided to set up a special headquarters in Shrewsbury, close to the Welsh border, from where the Special Branch itself could deploy its forces against the Welsh extremists. A highly experienced, and up to then successful policeman, the CID chief of Brixton, London, Commander Jock Wilson was to be brought in to overlord this fresh operation early in 1968, taking over from Detective-Supt. Vivian George Fisher. This special operation was eventually to engage the full-time services of more than three hundred detectives and many thousands of uniformed police and troops. The thrown-down gauntlet of challenge of the Welsh rebels had at last been taken up fully by the authorities.

Chapter Eighteen

A FTER THE BOMBING of the Temple of Peace and Health things quietened down for a short while. Then on January 6th 1968 an explosion damaged the newly built *Snowdonia Country Club* at the tiny village of Penisarwaun a few miles from Caernarfon in the county of Gwynedd, North Wales. At first it appeared that this could be classed as a purely local vendetta. A country club was not a likely target for extremists. Then the full story emerged. Mr Jack Nicks, a retired fruit wholesaler from Manchester had built the club in the grounds of his luxury home at Penisarwaun in the face of the total opposition of the local people. The Gwynedd cell of the MAC then decided to intervene...

"I realise that the Snowdonia club marked a move away from our usual targets of pipelines and government buildings. But this was in fact an attempt by a person from Manchester to install a country club in the face of all protest from the villagers of Penisarwaun. They had organised petitions and seen everybody, but, in spite of which this very wealthy man obviously had the council officials at Caernarfon well sewn up. He had planned this club knowing full well that it was of no benefit to the locals. They objected on the grounds that the roads through the village were very small, and could not take the late night transport which would be created. We saw this as a blatant example of everything we were fighting against. He was putting up this bloody club to cater for people of a like mind to himself in the middle of an environment to which it was completely alien.

"After talking about it, we decided that we'd show this bloke that money couldn't buy everything. It couldn't buy all the Welsh. Now he was living only a matter of maybe 25 yards from the premises, and we didn't want to physically damage anybody, not even him. So to frighten him off we decided to use only a small bomb. It would have been easy to demolish the place altogether, but we contented ourselves with just blowing all the doors and windows in… "

Despite intensive police enquiries no one was ever convicted for this offence. Local FWA men came under strong suspicion and two of them, Robert Jones and Edward Wilkinson were later each given a year's suspended sentence for unlawfully possessing explosives. Denis Coslett, the southern commandant was also under suspicion, but again nothing could be proved. Owain Williams was brought in for questioning, but in his case the affair escalated…

"There was this club blown up in Snowdonia. When it happened I was in London. I'd gone there to buy a Volvo car, leaving my father's car in Rhyl station and taking the train. While I was in London I read in the papers about the explosion, and that two guys had been arrested in Pen-y-Groes for it. I was living at the farm in Nefyn at the time, so I rang my mother and she said that the local police were looking for me, and were parked at the gates keeping the house under surveillance. I don't know whether these were CID or Special Branch, but apparently the weather was so cold and wet that one of them eventually caught pneumonia.

"Naturally I was worried, because these two arrested guys might have said I was involved or something. So I drove home in my new car, but on the way called on a girl I knew in Denbighshire, and taking her car we went to see if my father's car was still at the station in Rhyl. Being a chicken I didn't go into the station to check myself, but sent her. The car was still there, but all the tyres had been let down on it.

God knows by who! I went on to my home, but there were no police there, so I decided to make a tentative enquiry. I rang up the chief detective in Caernarfon, John Hughes, and asked what he wanted to talk to me about?

'Well, I just want a word with you, Williams. A couple of questions I'd like to ask you.'

'Well, you can ask me over the phone, can't you?'

'We'd rather see you,' he said very kindly.

'Oh, all right,' I told him. 'I'll whip in now then, and after that I can go home for supper.'

'Well, nooo. I suggest you eat your supper before you come.'

"Good job he said that, because I didn't come home for a hundred days. I was kept in Risley Remand centre for that length of time.

"I went driving so innocently into Caernarfon, 7 o'clock on a Sunday night. Only one light burning downstairs in the police station, nobody around. I stood there for a bit in the reception room, then shouted for someone to come. Suddenly all the lights came on and a gang of them closed around me.

'Ahh, we've got him now, the Big Fish!' they began to shout at me. 'You're the Big Fish! These other two are nothing, you're the one, the Big Fish!'

'I don't know what you're talking about,' I told them.

'Okay, take him upstairs!'

"I knew what that meant, the bloody naked bulb business. Once upstairs they began throwing me about the room from one to the other. Big fellows, shouting in my ears and trying to scare me. I was pretending that I wasn't impressed, but obviously I was... They said Wilkinson had done a statement, and Robert Jones had done a statement. I asked to see the statements please. This other guy from Anglesey has done one, John Gwilym Jones, they told me. . .

'Wilkinson bought some explosives from a quarryman in Llanllyfni and gave them to Robert Jones, who passed them to Gwilym Jones and he passed them to you. Three times this happened. Three packages, and there's been three explosions. The Temple of Peace, the pipelines at Llanrhaeadr and now the country club... '

"They questioned me from 7 at night until 5 in the morning, then locked me up. After a while two big fellows came into the cell. One took his coat off.

'John Hughes has gone home,' he said. 'We're free to work with you as we please.'

"One put his knee in my balls, and then I got a couple of kicks in the kidneys. I shouted and screamed at them.

'Why don't you punch me in the mouth? That'll be much better, I'll go to court in the morning with a nice mark... ' I was crapping myself, I was so scared, I kept thinking, '... a black eye will be better than a damaged kidney or crushed balls. Please God, they won't crush them, I'll lose my reputation.'

'Mr Hughes is a gentleman, and you talking to him like you did! We're not standing for that,' one of them kept telling me. 'What are you, a man or a mouse? Own up to what you've done.'

"They took me to court next day for a remand hearing, and these remands went on for a long time, nearly three months, and they'd got no evidence on me. No explosives, nothing. The other two lads had not implicated me, and John Gwilym Jones was a police plant who'd somehow infiltrated into the very early MAC organisation.

"When I was arrested I had a red card of the Patriotic Front on me, of which I was vice-president. At one stage Detective Glyn Owen threw it in front of me and said, very dramatically,

'Yes, Front it is too. Front for something far more sinister!'

He made a little sketch and speculated… 'Here we have Neil Jenkins, here Gethin Griffiths, here Cayo Evans, here Denis Coslett, and so-and-so here, and so-and-so here, and in the middle every time here's you like a bloody big spider!' I couldn't help but laugh, because of course it wasn't true.

"The same night they'd run an explosives check on my father's car. It was negative the first time, so they said they'd have another. They took a nitro-glycerine impregnated rag and rubbed it on the door-handles, the steering wheel, the boot handle, the gear lever, the window handles, but they put so much on, it looked suspicious. You see, when you drive a car how often do you open the back doors from the outside? Normally it's from the inside. Also, they'd forgot to put any on the handbrake. This was why I was acquitted, but that was a year later when I came to trial… Now, after nearly a hundred days on remand they bailed me, hoping I'd contact others, I'm sure Jock Wilson was behind this. I flew away, and they had Interpol after me… "

Interpol had indeed been alerted to track Owain Williams. In Bogota, Columbia, South America they approached Dewi Hughes, the son of the Welsh millionaire expatriate, Howell Hughes, known as a rabidly romantic Welsh nationalist. Dewi Hughes sent a letter to the Welsh newspaper *Y Cymro*, stating, "The gentlemen from Interpol have called at my hacienda and enquired if Owain Williams is staying here with me. No, he isn't, I've never heard of the man. But if Owain Williams should happen to drop in at any time, he will be most welcome here."

One story concerning Howell Hughes' enthusiastic nationalism, is of the time he attended an Eisteddfod in Wales, and was refused admittance because he had no ticket. He immediately produced a huge, long-barrelled revolver and held it to the doorkeeper's head. He was then allowed into the hall.

During the FWA trial at Swansea one of his emissaries presented each of the defendants with a Colombian Hundred Peso gold coin.

Interpol also searched Cayo Evans' mother's home in Marabella, Spain, and made extensive enquiries in Brittany, Belgium, Ireland and elsewhere. But it appeared that their quarry had successfully disappeared, at least for the time being…

Chapter Nineteen

1968 WAS TO PROVE the most intensive year for bomb attacks and other incidents, and to see an ever-increasing acceleration of security operations by the police and Special Branch. The winter months of 1967/68 were also to be a time of reorganisation for the Mudiad Amddiffyn Cymru, the MAC; and as a result of that re-grouping John Jenkins was to rise to the overall command…

"At this period my thoughts of the FWA were that since they had come out into the open, then by implication that barred them from very much effective action. Obviously the spotlight was on them, and they were going to be watched. This is the snag about Wales, there is very little you can do that goes unnoticed. I know they talk about big wide open spaces, but it's surprising how un-alone you are. Try stopping your car somewhere remote for any reason, and there is almost always someone around who is bound to see you.

"I considered our own organisation's thinking a bit silly on this point, that is until I started to make myself felt. They would say things like, 'We'll have a meeting. I'll meet you way upon top of the mountain, or in the forestry, or on a deserted beach.' This is nonsense; you're better to meet in middle of a crowded supermarket or something similar. I met a considerable amount of opposition from my colleagues when I tried to bring things like this in, and get it into a little more reasonably run operation.

"At this time we also had supply problems. Our main

stores of gelignite had folded up, it was all gone. The way it had been obtained was a very slipshod sort of arrangement. People had got the odd stick or two from various collieries and quarries, where people weren't too fussy about counting and storage.

But that wasn't good enough to run a campaign on, we needed a good store of stuff. So we had to make plans because nothing was coming through any more. Also we could no longer get our Venner time switches because we knew that the Special Branch were watching the limited outlets for them. The Electrical Boards had also changed over a period the time-switches which were in the lamp posts. Sometimes we could still find an old post which had one in, but nearly all had been changed from the manual to the electric switch, so we couldn't work them.

"I realised that I was obviously on my own. I clashed more and more with the members of the High Command because I wanted to get things done. Nothing was coming through, and they kept talking and talking and talking, and nothing was being done, nothing was coming. They would say, 'Oh yes, well I'll see… ' but that wasn't good enough. What we had to do was to get our supplies. We needed mechanisms, explosives and detonators.

"Fortunately I had friends in the south who were able to get me the detonators, so I had no problems about that at all. The next step was to get alternative timing mechanisms, so we developed our own based on alarm clocks… Take the glass off the clockface, drill a hole in it. Take either the positive/negative wire, strip the plastic from the end, insert the bared wire through the hole in the glass and tape it in. Remove the minute hand and shave the paint or covering from the hour hand so that a good connection is possible. Replace the glass ensuring that the wire through the glass is not touching any part of the clock. No matter how plastic the clock, the working parts are of metal, so connect the second positive/negative wire to the spindle, winding lever, whatever. From your battery run this second wire direct to the detonator in the gelignite. The wire via the clock is now parted by the hour hand and the inserted filament in the glass. When the hand moves round and touches the filament, the circuit is completed, and Bang! The circuits on these devices were always checked by using a bulb in place of the detonator, and by soldering all the connections for greater safety, so that if the clock was joggled there was no danger of an accidental circuit being created. All the parts, solder etc. could be bought over the counter at any large store.

"The next thing was to get the explosives. Through a sympathiser who worked there we knew that a colliery at Hafod near Wrexham was closing down, but that the magazine there was still fully stocked. These sympathisers were always to prove invaluable to us; normally they would be termed *sleepers*. Although not prepared to do something really active they could be counted on for supplying inside information and carrying out certain tasks. This man was able to tell us about the increased security measures that had been effected at all dynamite stores. In this particular store there was a built-in circuit which when the door was opened caused a warning light to flash on in the main colliery offices, which were manned night and day. Our sleeper was able to give us the times of watchmen's patrols etc, and most valuable of all, was able on the night of the operation to slip a piece of rubber between the circuit's contact points inside the stores so that when the door was to be opened, no light would come on in the offices.

"On the night in question, January 23rd 1968, myself and Alders drove to the colliery, allowing ourselves three hours for the operation. It was an easy matter to get the door open, and we took five cases of dynamite, totalling some 280 lbs.

Their accounting system must have been fairly hopeless because the most they could arrive at having been stolen was 150 lbs. But in fact I think each box contained 56 lbs. We took these to a temporary hiding place until I could transfer them to my dental-store at the barracks, and I was back at home within two hours.

"In an attempt to misdirect the police I had previously used a typewriter from a very frequented office, to type out part of a message which mentioned Bala, then burnt it partially leaving the section about Bala intact. This was left in the dynamite store in a place where they would have to look very hard, but should find it. They did in fact discover it, and apparently went rushing down to the Bala area, searching all over it for the gelignite.

"From now on I was for all practical purposes the commander of the Mudiad Amddiffyn Cymru. At councils when there was opposition my argument was that whatever they said was theory, whatever I said was practice. After all, I was speaking from strength. I had done these things and got away with them, therefore I had the key.

"I started off as commander with the same dual strategy that had already been decided upon, but with a flexibility which would allow for anything untoward or unexpected which might occur in the meantime. Once we had the explosives I began recruiting and setting up new cells of the MAC in various places. The system of operation was a very strong one, but paradoxically in that strength was its weakness. Whereby it was all bound up in one person, me... That is not personal conceit but a fact. This is why it all fell apart when I was eventually arrested. It was a question of security. It would be no good having a considerable number of people, which could be around fifty in number, knowing who's who, and what's what, and where's where. You can have this system, but it means that it only needs one person caught, perhaps one only on the fringes, and the whole damn lot goes in. The IRA have been proving this successfully over the last few years. We didn't base our cell system on them because to have done that would have been fatal. Every time an IRA man is arrested, within a few days a dozen more are pulled in. So we had to work on a system that no one knew anything.

"How it worked was that I would be the only person who knew who all our people were, and in each cell only one member of it would know me. He would know me by sight, but he wouldn't know what my name was, or where I lived, or anything else. I would get to know of potential cell leaders initially through contacts in the various extremist organisations, and at that time in Wales there were many active in some form or other. If a suitable recruit was found the word would be filtered back and I would go to look him over. He would be very carefully vetted and over a period of months I would act as the Devil's Advocate until I was satisfied that he was genuine. Then, and only then, I would personally train him and advise him how to set up his own cell. He could find his members, but we would vet them although they wouldn't know anybody else but their own cell leader. But the process of selection was initially a very long drawn one. Towards the end, because of the tremendously sophisticated and smothering Government counter-measures we needed new faces, and took a few chances.

"So, in every cell there would be one man who could give a description of me. That wouldn't help the police much, because it is difficult to imagine anyone who looks more commonplace than I am. Operationally, I would know each cell leader's whereabouts and when action was needed, and without telling anyone where I was going, I would call and see him without prior warning. Tell him whatever was necessary about the target etc. Leave him the stuff, and then go away and let him get on with it. I would always imply that there were others behind me and above me in the organisation, who would be watching him secretly to ensure that he carried out his orders.

"In my primary stages as commander I envisaged a triple-group structure, a propaganda group, a financial group, and the military group. The job of the financial was obviously to raise money. This could not be raised by covert means so it was necessary to use overt means, i.e. raffles, dances etc. — anything to get money for the cause. The other lot would be supposed to propagandise this through posters, leaflets etc. The military group was from the first to be the totally secret group. No one to know what they were, or who they were except me, because I was the chap running the military group.

"When we first started our campaign it was very successful. So successful that those others in finance and propaganda were no longer needed, they were finished, they couldn't move. The police were everywhere, they really couldn't move... and they had no means of contacting me unless I wished to go to them. I and my lot, the military group, carried on the fight alone. We had no help from the Irish or anyone else, we were our own people...

"I was approached through indirect sources during our campaign by the Bretons and asked to form an alliance. But since this would have meant increased security problems and no actual advantages in helping us to gain our objectives I regretfully turned it down, while taking care that the friendly links that already existed were maintained. We were told that we. could go across there at any time and be well taken care of. But the snag is that in order to do that one has to reveal oneself to people whom one doesn't really know.

"Another strange occurrence happened in 1968 re. the

question of alliances. The then famous agitator, Rudy the Red, came to London for a conference. He was only in London for about a day, then he suddenly disappeared from there, and turned up in the Swansea area. Nobody could understand what he was doing down there instead of being at the conference of students.

"The word filtered back to us that he wanted to contact the MAC, and that if we agreed with his proposals he was prepared to virtually give us a blank cheque… but! And the but was this, the blank cheque was coming from Eastern Germany, and the agreement would involve leaders of our organisation going to that country to learn new techniques, expertise etc. Well, one doesn't exchange a master in London for a master in Moscow, so we turned him down. I believe he approached other people too, but the next thing we heard was that he had applied for political asylum here, and had been turned down. This of course is not generally known, although I cannot understand why his application was such a secret. Maybe the authorities were worried because he had come to South Wales trying to contact Welsh revolutionaries. If that was so, then they needn't have been concerned. We weren't going to bite that apple, or any other apple offered by strangers. We were for Wales and the Welsh people, and intended to remain our own men… "

* * *

In the meantime the Parliamentarians of Westminster were contributing their share to the fight against the bombers. In the December 1967 edition of the glossy *Town* magazine there had appeared one of the by now standard-pattern articles about the Free Wales Army. In one of its paragraphs a man alleged to be a member of the Army was quoted as saying: "Nothing stops us. We have designs on all the traitors, Cledwyn Hughes, Emlyn Hooson, and all

POLICE HUNTING SABOTEUR

The wrecked section of the records block at the Inland Revenue offices at Llanishen.

Bomb destroys Cardiff tax-secrets offices

A bomb blast yesterday destroyed two offices in a Cardiff building where confidential tax records — including those of M.P.s and senior civil servants — are stored. People half-a-mile away heard the 2 a.m. blast at the single-storey block of Inland Revenue offices.

WESTERN MAIL REPORTER

A senior police officer said the explosion seemed deliberate. Names were not disclosed until the next of kin had been informed.

Yesterday's explosion, which shook houses some 200 yards away, amounted to destroying two record rooms in Block 3 of the St. Giles Road, Llanishen, Government office complex. No one was hurt.

Expert

Detectives cross-questioned David Shaws, head of Cardiff CID, who is leading police inquiries. The bomb represented only the danger to the use of an explosive device.

It was Office Service number...

One said an inland explosion expert named the building offices as damaged.

A Bomb Army Ordnance Corps bomb expert brought about 2lb. of explosive had been used.

He did not know whether the explosion was brought or home-made.

Only two fragments of the bomb had been found in the debris, said Mr. Shaw.

The walls of Office 3, each 3mft. by 12ft. thick and the corrugated roof were shown his ripping period credit. Two added a draught of shattered brickwork.

Nearby offices and windows in shed had glass that rained from the explosion gap.

Confidential papers were scattered over nearby bombed rooms, it made many messy. Bundles of bills were strong. The lost was heavy but no one was seriously alarmed.

A variety of road blocks was thrown around the city.

Motorists later knocked down part of the roof to make it safe and broke up a corridor roof. Plaster chunks were laid over the walls around the damaged office.

Mrs. Doris Dyke, who lives opposite her main gate of the offices, said she had gone to bed about before the explosion.

Loud bang

"It was a loud bang and the walls of the house shook," said Mrs. Dyke.

Mrs. Dyke said she did not see any people or any sound.

Her husband, Mr. W. A. Dyke, a nightwatch first overheard, found he had found office papers in his garden about the buildings from the area of the blast.

An Inland Revenue spokesman said last night that few people overheard something among the rubble today to find their many papers had been damaged, destroyed or lost.

He said the office was used for filing and no more had been there.

If any documents are found...

Editorial comment—Page 1

the traitors who have sold Wales out to England."

In the Commons, Mr Emlyn Hooson MP, the Liberal member for Montgomeryshire complained indignantly that words in the article constituted a breach of privilege of the House. During his address to Dr Horace King, the Speaker of the House of Commons, Mr Hooson quoted liberally from the article's text, claiming that, "In this article there is a threat on the life of the Secretary of State for Wales, and myself, and possibly others in continuation of their duties with their oath of allegiance to this House." He went on to say that the article declared, "The Free Wales Army would like to blow up the Severn Bridge!"

It being an acknowledged fact that many citizens of the United Kingdom desired in their secret hearts to blow up many things, including the House of Commons, Dr King sensibly ruled against the complaint of breach of privilege.

The very next action to be taken by the reconstituted Mudiad Amddiffyn Cymru has at times been an openly expressed desire of a great many otherwise respectable people... They blew up the Inland Revenue Offices on the outskirts of Cardiff.

At 2 a.m. in the morning of March 5th 1968, two confidential tax record offices at Spur J in Block 3 at the Tŷ Glas Road, Llanishen Government office complex were blown to pieces; and the painstaking work of Inland Revenue officers scattered to the winds.

Frederick Ernest Alders, the young lieutenant of John Jenkins, was very much involved in the preliminary stages of this action...

"At the beginning of March 1968, John and myself arranged to visit South Wales. We stayed overnight at John's mother's house and next morning drove on into Cardiff. We picked up a man who was a stranger to me, but who knew John. He took us to a house in the city where we met another fellow whose name was Hiscocks. He lived at Llanishen and knew the layout of the Government buildings there. I was driving the van and the others talked. They were discussing the best means of access to the tax record offices. We drove round the complex to its rear where there was a waste area of marshy ground. But John rejected this approach for several reasons after the four of us had looked it over, and we got back into the van again. Hiscocks noticed the *L* plates on the van, and he suggested that the best way to get to the tax offices was through the front gate. The buildings covered a very big area and he said that a lot of learner drivers used to go inside and practise their three point turns and reversing.

"Hiscocks directed us through the gate and we went quite a way until we came to some prefabricated blocks. While I did three point turns etc., the others took a good look at the place. Hiscocks said he'd worked there at one time and he pointed out the exact location of the record offices. After a while we went back into Cardiff and dropped off the stranger and Hiscocks, then returned to North Wales… "

The 4th of March was the occasion of the Wales-France rugby match at Arms Park, and during the days preceding the match an estimated 70,000 fans flocked into the city, among them many thousands of Bretons and Frenchmen. The night of the match was a busy time for the police with thousands of roistering Welshmen and Frenchmen packing the pubs and clubs of Cardiff. A solitary figure carrying a haversack on his shoulder climbed the compound fence at Llanishen and made directly for the tax offices. Carefully breaking out one corner of the window he placed the haversack inside the room and then made his way cautiously back along the route he had come. At 2 a.m. Sunday morning the bomb inside the haversack roared and the operation was successfully completed.

This attack against the Inland Revenue caused a furore in the Government. Welsh MPs on all sides denounced the outrage, and never had there been such unity among them for bringing the culprits to book. Questions were tabled to be put to the Home Secretary and a motion deploring the incident and calling on the House of Commons to condemn it was prepared. The Secretary of State for Wales, the unhappy Cledwyn Hughes stated, "All but the tiniest minority of people in Wales will join me in condemning the motives which inspired the blowing up of the Inland Revenue offices in Llanishen, Cardiff… "

What was very noticeable by absence were the confident assurances of early arrest and conviction of the bombers, which up to now had been the norm. Again the extensive enquiries of the police made no headway, and to rub salt into their figurative wounds two more blasts were shortly to shake Wales during what was to be for the bombers, a Merry Month of May.

Chapter Twenty

"Tramp tramp tramp the boys are marching
To join up with the FWA
Beneath the Union Jack we never will be free,
So strike a blow for Wales and liberty… "

That ever irritating and very visible thorn in the flesh of the authorities, the uniformed Free Wales Army, was also marching on its merry way. Since the spotlight of publicity was constantly centred upon them they became a prime target for the police, and a focus of hero-worship for many young and old people all across the Principality. The soldiers of the various columns played to their audience. In pubs and clubs, at village dances and fairs, the squads of green uniforms would make their appearance. Sometimes the para-military rigouts would cause resentment and lead to brawls, as on one occasion in a Chinese restaurant in Caerfyrddin.

Cayo Evans, Denis Coslett and a third man, all uniformed, were enjoying a meal, when the door opened and four RAF men came in. The largest of the four kept staring at the FWA men with mock wonder and hectoring them, repeating at intervals in a loud voice, "What the fucking hell is that?"

Still chewing his Chicken Chow Mein, Denis Coslett removed his spectacles and laid them by the side of his plate, got to his feet and walked up to the large airman. Then, without a word being said, knocked him down with a wicked right hook. Within seconds the restaurant was a brawling mass of green and blue uniforms locked in combat, and the diminutive Chinese cooks and waiters lashing out at both sides indiscriminately with their kitchen utensils.

On several other occasions the hot-tempered Coslett was embroiled with opponents who had jeered at his group. Cayo Evans also found himself involved in fights because of his very well known FWA affiliations, as did a lot of the uniformed nationalists.

These street and bar brawls served one useful purpose however, in that they demonstrated that the FWA could not be harrassed with impunity by corner bullyboys or political thugs. Police harrassment could not be countered so easily. Many FWA members found themselves in court for minor offences that in most areas would previously have been winked at and let pass with a warning by the local constable. Inevitably situations arose when violent clashes took place between the police and the FWA.

The local Borough elections were held in Llanelli in early May 1968. On the 9th May Denis Coslett was on the forecourt of the Town Hall to hear the results announced. Following his usual custom he was wearing his uniform, and was approached by a policeman. As always in these cases there are two versions of the story. This is the FWA version as related by Denis Coslett.

"I was outside the Town Hall and a policeman, (PC D.J. Jones) very tall and lanky, I've seen more meat on a bicycle chain, told me,

'Take that badge off,' pointing at my FWA flash. I pointed to his helmet plate, and said.

'You take that Imperialist badge off.'

'You know your badge is illegal,' the policeman said, and pushed me hard in the chest … I had to jump up to hit him, he was so tall."

More police came and dragged Coslett into a police car.

The fight continued en-route and at one stage the car nearly crashed when the prisoner managed to grab the driver's neck. Once at the police station Coslett held onto the car door with both hands while the officers tried to wrench him loose. The door groaned and came off at the hinges. The police then dragged him into the corridor and in the struggle his head smashed through the glass of one of the interior windows. They threw him into a cell and left him for an hour. Then several officers came down to the cell and opened the door. The following dialogue ensued…

"Cooled down, have you?"

"You sod off from here! Why don't you come one at a time?"

"Take your boots off."

"You try and take them off."

"Take your jacket off."

"You try and take it off."

"Alright… We're going to hammer you… We're going to paste the living daylights out of you."

Denis Coslett says: "Well, discretion being the better part of valour, I thought I might as well take the coat off. As I did so one of them came at me. The fight started again and I was taking a hell of a hammering, when from the corridor a policewoman screamed… 'OH MY GOD! You've put his eye out! You've put his eye out!'"

One punch had knocked Denis' glass eye from its socket and as it bounced on the floor she had seen it and took it for a real one… The police immediately left him alone, still wearing his boots.

Denis Coslett was later fined £25 by Llanelli magistrates for assaulting a police officer. A charge of wilfully damaging a window at Llanelli Police Station was dismissed…

*   *   *

The same police station was to prove a useful hiding place for the FWA later that summer, and again Denis Coslett featured prominently. He and another member of his column managed through friends to obtain the use of a very powerful camera. They hired a helicopter and flew over the major water installations of the Elan Valley, Tryweryn, Clywedog etc. and took some 90 pictures of likely target areas. The police got wind of this and instigated the usual house searches but found nothing. The pictures were hidden in Llanelli police station by a friendly contact there.

By now the Special Branch were heavily involved in the hunt for the saboteurs, and because of their prominence in the FWA, Denis Coslett and Cayo Evans saw more of these crack invest-igators than most nationalists. One incident has always remained vividly in Coslett's memory ....

"One evening Cayo and myself came down from Bont to my then home in Brynhyfryd. We noticed that a Special Branch car was following us. We went into the house for some tea and after a while a knock came at the door. It was my driver/bodyguard, a huge man we nick-named *The Gorilla*.

'I've got it here,' he said, tapping his pocket.

'What have you got there?' I asked.

'I'd got it hidden in the chimney of a derelict house,' he told me. 'But I found the kids had pulled it down and were kicking it about the floor... So I thought I'd better bring it to you.'

'Bring me what?'

'The gelignite!'

'Well thank you very much, the Special Branch is down by there... You just keep it in your pocket, because I don't want to know.'

The Gorilla's face was a blank. 'Well what am I going to

do with them. There's nearly a dozen sticks.'

'Start eating them as far as I'm concerned!' I shouted. 'Eat the bloody things!'

"Of course I couldn't leave them with him, but we couldn't try hiding them in the house either, not with the SB's sitting outside, and for all we knew coming in at any second with a search warrant. So we decided to try a bluff. He kept the gelignite in his pocket and the three of us went out to Cayo's Volkswagen car. In the bonnet was a massive pair of cow horns which he was delivering to somebody or other. We drove out to the main road, and straight away one car came in front; and another behind, sandwiching us and forcing a halt.

'Right boys, let's have a look in your car.' The detective was grinning all over his face.

'Oh don't open that bonnet!' Cayo begged, acting very scared. 'Don't mess around, in that bonnet, it's dangerous.'

"The detective was really happy now. He opens the bonnet and shone his torch inside, then swore. 'A pair of fucking cow's horns! Fucking horns! Go on Evans, get off. Get off out of my sight!' He was so disgusted he didn't even think to make a body search, and away we went with the geli still in the *Gorilla's* pocket... "

*   *   *

A more sinister note was struck in an attempt by Left-wing activists to takeover the FWA. A group of men from Cardiff contacted Cayo Evans, claiming that they had formed a column of the FWA, that they had all their arms and equipment, and wanted to control the southern areas of Wales. Upon the customary checks being made it was found that although on the surface they appeared genuine, their printed material, badges and other equipment were all of a very costly nature. Suspicion was aroused because the FWA commandants could not understand from where the large amounts of money necessary for items of this quality were raised. After further investigation the group turned out to be all full-time Communist Party members. Since the FWA was very anti-communist, the group was rebuffed and warned off.

Tony Lewis had experience of another type of infiltration, that of the agent-provocateur. "During the time we were running the Patriotic Front we received many offers of help. People would write or phone us saying that they had been in the army and had used explosives etc. and any time we wanted help or military training they would oblige. As I said before, I was more involved with the political wing, but I was always prepared if it became necessary, to try and fight. We were always hoping something would happen as in Ireland where the police and troops press against the people. If they'd started something like that against us we would have been prepared to head for the mountains and attempt to start a guerrilla campaign.

"What I did try to do in anticipation of this ever happening was to arrange through parts of Wales various safe spots where guerrillas could hide out, and find blankets, stores etc., stay a night or two, and then move on. I had quite a lot of these fixed up. But as I explained to people who wanted to give us the safe houses, we preferred sheds, or barns etc. because at this time the police were really ripping out the houses of nationalists in their searches for explosives and arms.

"Personally I was not pushed about too badly by the police, but I was forever being arrested and brought to the police station for questioning. I remember one day a fellow who had come to work on the buses — I was a bus driver at the time — this fellow was a Scotsman who came to work as a conductor. The strange thing was he was a petty criminal with convictions, yet he got the job. Normally a conviction would be enough to debar a man from this type of work. Anyway, he said he was a staunch Scottish Nationalist, and for two or three weeks he talked to me about this, knowing my own views.

"One day he came to me with a detonator, which he said he'd picked up, and asked me if I could use it. I'd never seen one before and was curious so I shoved it in my pocket meaning to store it away somewhere later, and went on with my work. I arrived home during mid-evening and had no sooner got into the house when the police were at the door to arrest me and take me in for questioning.

"Well, there I am with this detonator still in my pocket, and there was no chance to dispose of it. I couldn't even chuck it through the window because they were standing around me. I went to the toilet hoping to dispose of it but one of them came with me. All I could manage was to push it into my sock. They took me in the car, I wasn't handcuffed or anything, and I thought perhaps I might be able to hide it somewhere in the police station, a filing cabinet or similar.

"At the station they sat me down near to a gas fire, it was very cold outside, and I was happy to get close to the fire.

"We all sit down, they're questioning me and I've got one leg crossed over the other, very much at ease, when I realised that this detonator was getting very hot! I thought, 'Christ Almighty!' Sweating with fear I moved my leg very quietly and put it back on the floor, then kept trying to unobtrusively wriggle my body as far from the fire as I could, and all the time the police are questioning and questioning, and I'm wriggling and wriggling, and getting more and more frightened and the bloody detonator is getting hotter and hotter.

"I knew that technically they couldn't body-search me without they charge me; however they sometimes did. But that night I wasn't being arrested for something naughty like a bomb going off or something similar. They would really pull me about on those occasions. Obviously they had pulled me in this time in hopes of finding the detonator, because while I was in the station they searched my house like a fine tooth comb. At last they released me, and I was never so glad of anything in my life than to get out into that freezing cold air. Very shortly after this incident the Scotsman left the buses. To me it seemed obvious that this petty crook had been told what to do. Perhaps he wasn't a police agent as such, but maybe they had something on him and had been told that if he co-operated with them they would forget all about it."

Chapter Twenty One

O N THE 2ND MAY 1968 the secret Mudiad Amddiffyn Cymru for the first time stepped briefly out of the shadows. Three journalists, Mr Harold Pendlebury of the *Daily Mail*, Mr Ian Skidmore, also employed by that newspaper, and Mr Emyr Jones of the *Wrexham Leader*, came face to face with the commander of the MAC, John Jenkins.

Ever aware of the power of the media John Jenkins had known that eventually in some way or other he must attempt to make his organisation's aims known to a national publicity outlet. As he had previously said: "I could of course envisage a military confrontation with the English. But I wasn't trying to do that. All I was trying to do at this time was, as Mao put it, 'Make people take the initial step of a thousand miles march.' To make them think! To alter the political temperature by just a few degrees, so that they would then be responsive to nationalist propaganda, and to try and counter the other side's propaganda.

"I quite obviously could not hope to take the mass of the Welsh people through the whole thing of making them responsive up to the point of actually bearing arms, and the fight that would follow. I couldn't hope to succeed in that. All I could do was to try to get them off their backsides and make them actually listen… I had some degree of success in this by using the mass media. Tryweryn was big news here in Wales, but no one in England had ever heard of it — until the pipelines started to go, and then they all heard about it.

"The mass media was the same machine that was being

used against us, but we succeeded in turning it to our advantage. You see, once Fleet Street uses a story, it comes into Wales in the mass circulation papers, and then the ordinary Welsh become conscious of the story. That's the way we had to go about it. First impress the story on Fleet Street, and in turn they will impress it upon the ordinary Welsh. You can only impress from the top downwards, never from the bottom up.

"We had a deadline for our aims, and that deadline was the Investiture. You must understand why the Investiture was to take place, as it had before for the first time ever in 1911. It took place in 1911 because the Government of the time was in great disfavour with the people of Wales. Lloyd George needed something urgently to demonstrate that he was at least the leader of the Welsh people. He stood to rise or fall by it. So, ergo, the Investiture. The same thing was to happen in 1969. It was to be a polariser of opinion which was to swing that public opinion over in favour of the existing set up, or at least to keep it at the status quo. Well, opinion polarisers can be used in two different ways, and we wanted to swing that opinion our way.

"The interview with Skidmore and Pendlebury was an essential part of that campaign strategy. Part of the attempt to bring down retribution. We had to show our credentials and make the threat against Prince Charles so that the authorities, by overreacting would embitter the average Welshman against them.

"We got hold of Jones, the *Wrexham Leader* journalist. Initially we had virtually to kidnap him because of course he was nothing to do with us. We took him way up into the mountains and explained to him what we wanted done. You see we knew where he was from, and we knew his family, and we were able to use threats against him and them. Which wouldn't have been carried out, but he wasn't to know that.

He believed us, and was naturally very worried. One doesn't like doing these things, but our security system was essential.

"He then contacted Skidmore and Pendlebury, who had already put the word out that they were seeking an interview, and told them that he had fixed a meeting. They were to be at the *Vaults* bar at Chester at a certain time, and someone would appear and tell them where the actual venue of the interview was to be. We had already scouted around and decided to hold that interview at Skidmore's own home, a manor house called Picton Hall near Mickle Trafford, a few miles from Chester. Which was an ideal site for the job.

"We had to make sure however that no people were following, or knew anything at all about it. This was the first time that the MAC had ever made any statement of any sort to anybody, so obviously it was a scoop as far as Pendlebury and Skidmore were concerned.

"I went personally into the pub, and unnoticed by the three journalists had a drink at the bar, which was fairly crowded, and took a good look at them so that I would know their faces. Then I left to join my other two men outside, Alders and Roberts. I phoned up the pub and asked for Emyr Jones. When he came on I told him to take his companions from the pub, not telling them anything because he was being watched by us, then drive slowly in the general direction of Skidmore's home. When they reached Mickle Trafford, and only then, he could tell them that the interview was to be held at Picton Hall. This way the men in the car would not really have any opportunity of contacting others.

"The main road from Chester is rather narrow and to reach Skidmore's home it was necessary to leave the main road on the left, drive down a lane and turn left again into the Hall's entrance. On the corner of this lane is a telephone box. After watching the journalists leave the pub and drive off slowly, we followed in our car, overtook them and went on at speed. I got out at the telephone box and stood back in the shadows while my two friends went on and parked the car around a bend, then went themselves up to the Hall. As soon as the reporters' car reached the entrance to the house, Alders and Roberts jumped them, making believe that they were armed. Alders got straight into the journalists' car and drove it off, the other chap got the three men into the house and held them there. While Alders went away in the opposite direction I waited and watched to see if anyone was following him. After half an hour he came back to the Hall, and with the other chap shepherded the journalists into the darkened lounge. No lights were on at all. When all is ready he then phones me at the kiosk, because by then we know that there is no one following, that the three men are on their own. I pick up our car and come on to the house.

"We had originally intended to use a small spotlight in the lounge, but that gave out too much reflected glare. So I told them to put it out, and we used only a tiny pentorch for the three to take their notes by. What I did then was to describe all the jobs we'd done up to that point in great detail, so that whoever was to hear about this would know that we were serious. Because this interview wasn't primarily intended for the readers of the *Daily Mail*: it was meant for the Special Branch. The object of the exercise was to give those gentlemen our credentials, and impress them with our will. But we didn't want to do it with bandoliers over our chests and hand-grenades hanging from our belts. We thought we should do it this way, with total understatement to impress them that we meant to do what we said. Such as when they asked me… 'Are you threatening to kill Prince Charles? ' I replied… 'No, no, no, I am simply saying that we cannot guarantee his protection when he sets foot in Wales.'

"It was all very quiet, matter of fact, and understated...
And those journalists bloody well loved it! I couldn't get
from there. They were giving out bottles of wine, they were
giving us lists of names, places, coming events — they
wanted us to do things!

"Of course, when they got this information, details that
even the police didn't know, it was marvellous stuff for them.
They go rushing back to their editor, and naturally he
immediately gets on to whoever he gets on to, and within
hours in comes the Special Branch and the reporters go
straight in for questioning, and are really put through the
ringer... What emerged from it, is that everything was really
tightened up then from a security angle. Because as far as
the authorities are concerned we have demonstrated that
we have the means, the will and the power to kill the
Prince... and that did it! Nationalists were followed,
investigations were intensified, if you even go behind a bush
in Wales to pee, there is a Special Branch man. They pulled
all the stops out, and from our point of view it worked like
a dream.

"No one had any intention of killing the Prince. Can you
imagine all the mothers of Wales if we did that? They would
be up in arms against us. But the threat meant that the Special
Branch would pressure Welsh people, and Welsh people
would turn against them.

"We knew our scheme had worked, and that our threats
had gone home, because the news was suppressed. If the
interview hadn't been suppressed we would have worried,
because then we would have known that the authorities
thought our threats were empty ones, and that there was
nothing to be concerned about. That's how we knew we had
succeeded, they clamped a 'D' notice on the whole lot. The
only mention of the interview was a front page headline in
the *Daily Mirror*, 'Threat to Prince. Life in Danger,' but no

details, just an account that a secret interview had taken place. No one knew anything. As I said, if they had released the details we would have considered that they disregarded us. Ironically, I had been four hours with those reporters, talking about the MAC's aims, motivations, etc. The reporters took a full account, but the only things ever used, were those used against me at my trial… "

During John Jenkins' trial, Mr Tasker Watkins QC, for the prosecution referred to the interview, calling it a "rather strange and almost macabre event," and said that the police had been concerned to discover who had been present. Mr Tasker Watkins also said that soon after the interview the journalists published much of the material they gathered. The Queen's Counsel neglected to mention just which newspapers had published the material, and why there had been delay in using such a scoop.

Chapter Twenty Two

THE WELSH OFFICE, the mini-Whitehall of Wales, is part of Crown Buildings, Cathays Park, Cardiff, in the same area as the new police headquarters and the Temple of Peace. One suite of its offices was for the use of the recently appointed Secretary of State for Wales, Mr George Thomas, MP for Cardiff West, who had replaced Cledwyn Hughes. Mr Thomas was a forceful and determined character, who on his appointment had gone on television and announced that he would be standing no nonsense from Welsh extremists. "In fact, I believe the period of violence is now over," he added.

The Mudiad Amddiffyn Cymru decided to show the politician the fallacy of that statement. Because the intensive police activity in the Principality's capital city had necessitated a temporary de-activation of the MAC's Cardiff cell, it was decided to treat this action as a combined operation and bring in men of the Free Wales Army, Swansea column to carry out the actual attack on the Welsh Office, although the preliminary reconnaissance of the building and the supplying of the bomb would be the responsibility of MAC. The selected target area was a window below street level under a short concrete footbridge leading to the east entrance of the Welsh Office. With this target area they could guarantee extensive damage to George Thomas' personal suite of offices, and thus get their message home to that gentleman with additional impact.

The most difficult part of the operation was its timing.

Since the bombing of the Temple of Peace police patrolling of the area had been stepped up, and the possibility of a wandering policeman being killed was a real one. To avoid this potentially damaging propaganda-wise event occurring, a very detailed plan was devised which although increasing the risk to the bombers, would almost certainly ensure no unwanted loss of life.

The bomb, contained in a haversack and comprising 15lbs of Belex gelignite taped around an empty metal canister, with the usual dry-cell batteries, detonator and a fortuitously acquired Venner time-switch, was made up in Cardiff. Two Swansea men came by car and picked up the bomb during the evening of May 24th 1968.

At 2.30 a.m. the following morning the two men drove carefully through the streets of Cardiff heading for Cathays Park, the deadly package lodged securely on the car floor behind the driver. Cruising around the edges of Cathays Park the car halted when all was clear, and one man slipped out, took the bomb and headed into the darkness where the shrubs and flowers of the park afforded a shadowed shelter. The car immediately drove away.

The bomber lay in the deepest shadow of the buildings before him. At 2.58 a.m. exactly he set the timing mechanism in motion, allowing 30 minutes to contact point, then once more settled himself to wait. At 3.20 a.m. on the northern edges of the city a member of the Cardiff MAC cell slipped from his home and went to the phone kiosk at the corner of the slumbering street. He dialled 999 and when the police answered reported that there had been a shooting and that the gunman was running amok in an area some three miles from the city centre; then he rang off.

Within seconds police cars were switched from their normal patrols to the scene of the reported incident. The watcher in Cathays Park saw the area patrol car roar away, and sprinted across the intervening space. He reached the building, dropped down to the forecourt and ducked under the covered concrete runway. It took only seconds to place the bomb, then he hauled himself back up to street level and again disappeared into the darkness of the park, where throwing himself flat to the earth he waited.

At precisely 3.28 a.m. the bomb roared and 36 offices, including the suite of the Secretary of State were badly damaged, hundreds of plate-glass windows shattered, doors ripped from their hinges, chunks of masonry hurled hundreds of yards. Even before the echoes of the blast had died the bomber was up and running towards his cruising getaway car, which had only then reappeared. Without the vehicle stopping the bomber wrenched open the passenger door and was inside. They then went straight to the house of a sympathiser, close to the city centre, and remained quietly indoors for two days until the furore had abated and they were able to travel sedately homewards.

As always the police reacted with swift efficiency to the bombing. Within brief minutes of the explosion all major road and rail exits from the city were sealed. Vehicles stopped and searched, drivers, pedestrians, rail and coach passengers questioned. The homes of all known FWA men and extreme nationalists in the Cardiff area were raided, and as extra police were drafted in, the search widened to include other areas. But once again the security system of the extremists proved foolproof, and no one was ever charged with, or convicted of the offence.

The recently appointed George Thomas was awakened at his home some miles away, and told of the explosion. Later, at Llandudno, he momentarily vented his spleen. "The nationalists of Wales have created a monster they cannot control," he shrilled. "The anonymous cowards who slunk away this morning are a disgrace to the Welsh people."

Gwynfor Evans, Welsh Nationalist MP was quick to counter-attack, saying that he was disgusted at the irate Mr Thomas' blatant exploitation of the explosion for party political ends. He went on to again accuse the British Secret Service... " They (the explosions) are the work of the Secret Service, who want to do the maximum damage to Plaid Cymru. This sounds fantastic; but should not be ruled out!"

Inevitably it was a race between police and reporters as to whom could interview the FWA commandants first.

Cayo Evans stated that he was thankful that no one had been injured. But warned that more explosions would follow until Welshmen ruled Wales.

Denis Coslett, in a televised interview, went a little further. He warned the then Prime Minister, Harold Wilson, that as well as bombings there would be open insurrection unless Home Rule talks for Wales were begun.

As if to underline these warnings, within less than 48 hours, early in the morning of May 27th, another bomb exploded at the Lake Fyrnwy Dam in Montgomeryshire, causing damage to a reserve pipeline.

If this further explosion embarrassed George Thomas MP, the fact was that what had been planned instead of the Lake Fyrnwy bombing would have caused the Secretary of State a far greater intensity of embarrassment. John Jenkins as commander of the MAC knew the planned date of the projected Welsh Office operation.

"I thought this was fine, it fitted in nicely with something I had planned. Princess Margaret was due to come to Wales and open a new Shirehall in Mold, Flintshire. We were going to do a job on the Shirehall. What we intended was to drive openly in the daytime up to the Shirehall entrance the day before the Princess' visit, when all the decorative preparations would be going on. We would be using a van and be dressed in coucil employee overalls. From previous reconnaissance we knew that the Shirehall entrance was unguarded, so we intended to lift two ornamental trees in tubs and place them one each side of the entrance. In each tub would be a bomb timed to explode at three in the morning. The front of the new building is all glass, so you can imagine the mess that would greet the Princess when she came next morning to officially open the place. George Thomas of course was scheduled to be with her, so it would also have served as our self-introduction to him personally.

"Unfortunately the Welsh Office operation was carried out two or three nights in advance of the original plan. This meant that security at Mold became straight away so tight that it was impossible to get near the place. Rather then waste the opportunity to greet visiting Royalty with an explosion, we caused the Fyrnwy explosion. Not one of our better efforts, I must admit."

The next effort of the MAC was to be emphatically one of their better ones...

*   *   *

Prince Charles and his father, The Duke of Edinburgh, were to visit South Wales on Friday 28th June 1968 for an informal one day tour of four towns, Llanelli, Port Talbot, Swansea and Cardiff. All police leave in those towns was cancelled for the occasion and extra squads of Special Branch and Regional Crime Squad detectives drafted into key points. The *Daily Express* journalist, John Christopher, reassured his readers in the previous Monday's edition of his paper that the five men believed responsible for the Cardiff bombs were being watched night and day by detectives. The five were not Welsh nationalists, he wrote, or members of the undercover Free Wales Army, they acted entirely on their own, and at least one was an explosives expert. John Christopher quoted a senior police officer as saying, "These men are very dangerous. But we are quite happy with the progress we have made on the enquiry. It is likely that arrests will be made in connection with the bomb outrages in the next few weeks."

It is to be hoped that the journalist's display of inside knowledge did something to ease any devoted royalists' worries as to how the Royal duo would be welcomed in Wales. The official preparations for that welcome were already in full swing. As were the welcomes planned by various extremist groups, including the Mudiad Amddiffyn Cymru led by John Jenkins...

"The job at Helsby came about because Prince Charles was coming to Cardiff to do some public relations prior to the Investiture. We had heard that in Cardiff there would be hostile demonstrations to meet him. This would of course attract the attention of the Special Branch, and they would be expecting more to happen down there. For us, it was a good opportunity to blow a pipeline elsewhere.

"The pipeline chosen after extensive recce's was Helsby near Hapsford in Cheshire. The spot was where the pipeline emerges from underground and crosses the main railway line between Chester and Manchester. (The 25 mile, 60 inch pipe carried 30 million gallons of water a day from a treatment works on the River Dee at Huntington, 3 miles south of Chester, to the Liverpool pumping station at Prescot.)

"We went up there at night, myself, Alders and our driver. The routine with the car was that it would continue moving while the job was carried out, and return at pre-arranged intervals to the pick-up point, never actually halting or even slowing unless we were waiting. If for some reason or other we were not at the pick-up point the car driver was always to carry on past and return later after the pre-arranged interval had elapsed. It was always essential that exact times were strictly adhered to.

"We had done the usual exhaustive checks about the passing of trains, passenger, freight etc., and we were going to select a time of explosion which would be just between the passing of a passenger and a freight train. The beauty of this job, from a demolition point of view, was that right under the pipe, which was very thick and very wide, was a large concrete abutment to secure the bank.

"About four hundred yards from the spot we left the car and made our way on foot. Steel can't be fractured of course, and this pipe was about two inches thick steel. This needs a much greater punch and impact over a much smaller area to penetrate it than for example, cast iron. There was a nine inch gap between the concrete and the pipe and it had worked out that a minimum of 15lbs of explosive would be needed. To be on the safe side I used in actual fact 17lbs of Polar Ammon dynamite.

"It was necessary to place the bomb very carefully. Had it been set an inch or so either side it would merely have gouged a scratch. We took a long time over the placing. We were unable to drill for security reasons, so it became a question of precision arrangement of the explosives so that the blast would go straight up and not sideways. Once the bomb was set, we walked back to the pick-up point. The car came at the prearranged time, and we were away.

"The bomb went off and blew a large hole, I think about 15 inches width, which was a large one for two inch steel. We had laid the geli beautifully and blew the hole right under the middle of the pipe, which, as was later admitted, the authorities didn't think possible. For that reason they hadn't bothered to remove the concrete. What turned out to make the blast even more effective was that the freight train was late coming along, five minutes later than it should have been. This meant that as it neared the spot where the bomb had blown, the water had had an extra five minutes to become high and flooding. The train got stuck in it, but no one was hurt, thank God. But in the meantime the water was smashing down on the concrete abutment and being hurled a hundred yards into the air to fall on a big field of corn which was all flattened... How much the farmer claimed for that in his insurance is anybody's guess.

"Next day they sent squads of detectives down to look for clues, of which the water had ensured there were none to be found. They also sent a gang of about two hundred Paddies to clear up the mess. The tracks and ballast had all been washed away, and as luck would have it the following day when the navvies arrived there was the worst rainstorm for years, which compounded the damage, since everything they tried to dump was doubly inundated. The water had to be switched off because of the harm this huge falling was doing to roads, banks etc., and I believe it remained off for six weeks.

"One man did gain from the explosion however, a classic case of the ill-wind bringing someone good. This was the landlord of the pub which directly overlooked the pipe. Not even a window was smashed in the building, and imagine, two hundred thirsty navvies on his doorstep!

"The *Western Mail* on the front page next day was filled with the story of the pipeline blast, the Cardiff demonstrations, the smoke bombs, the lot! No one, I think, had to ask what the significance of it all was, not this time."

* * *

The demonstration at Cardiff took place on the day of the Helsby bombing outside the Welsh Office. Approximately 200 anti-investiture supporters mainly from the Patriotic Front and the Welsh Language Society were among the crowd waiting to welcome the Prince. The police had erected barriers to confine the crowd, and when the young Prince left the Welsh Office, accompanied by the usual entourage of local dignitaries, security men and hangers-on, all was under control. The demonstrators began booing and waving their protest placards, and with a display of considerable courage Prince Charles left his escort and alone approached the hostile sections.

In a verbal exchange with one demonstrator, Murray Jenkins of the Welsh Language Society, the Prince admitted,

"I'm not too well up on Welsh history."

"I'll accept that," Murray Jenkins told him. "You are not very bright."

Mr George Thomas, who had scurried to the barriers, was quick to champion his prince. "He is, you know. He's going to University."

Murray Jenkins was unabashed. "Yes, he's getting into University on two very poor 'A' levels."

At this interesting stage in the exchange, when all were racking their brains for further cutting remarks to make, the smoke bombs starting falling, belching out clouds of acrid fumes. The feathers in the cocked hat of the Lord Lieutenant shook wildly as he danced about trying to stamp on the evil-smelling cylinders; while like a modern Raleigh, a senior police officer removed his cloak to hurl it upon one of the bombs. Fights broke out in the crowd between loyalists and anti-royalists, and at one stage several people were heaped together in one squirming mass upon the ground. Police went in and arrests took place. But not everyone present took it as light-heartedly as the Prince himself appeared to do. Keith Griffiths was one for whom the demonstration held serious intent...

"At this time I was very concerned with organising the

street demo's and confrontations with the police. I wanted as many as possible. One of the most successful was the Welsh Office. At least two hundred of us were there. Four of us from the Patriotic Front had the smoke bombs. As soon as I arrived there I was spotted by the police. We knew all the Welsh ones from the Regional Crime Squads. One got behind me, a detective, or probably Special Branch at this time. I had my bomb down my trouser leg, and this big hefty policeman was standing right behind me. So I lit a cigarette and let the tip go down on the bomb's touch-paper. When I realised it was alight I threw it. Immediately I did that he grabbed me and swung me round. I swung a rather ineffectual punch at him, because he was a big bloke remember, and the next moment the uniformed police were in. I was grabbed and had my legs pulled right apart and thumped in the kidneys while taken to the van.

"There was a uniformed policeman in the van, a Welsh speaker who began to talk to me; and I couldn't reply because I didn't speak Welsh at that time. He seemed quite sympathetic, as far as they go. Then a plain-clothes man jumped in, a thug of a character. He started berating me, and he was red in the face. Obviously we'd embarrassed them, because if anyone had had a real bomb there, Charles would have been dead. We'd proved that their security was useless. I argued back and he proceeded to bang me about the head, he was really upset, much to the embarrassment of this Welsh-speaking policeman, who just sat there going redder and redder. Then they took me down to the station and charged me…"

Keith Griffiths was fined £20 after pleading guilty to using threatening behaviour whereby a breach of the peace was likely to be occasioned in College Rd., Cathays Park, Cardiff.

Chapter Twenty Three

THE NATIONAL MILITARY ORGANISATION

Volunteers of the Army are required to report to Llanwrtyd Wells on Saturday, August the 31st 1968.

There will be a general meeting and training session of volunteers of all commands at a pre-arranged place to which you will be taken on the above date.

Come prepared to spend some nights in camp. Bring ground-sheet, blankets or sleeping bag, tent if you have one, and combat uniform or other suitable clothing.

You shall need enough food for four to six meals (48 hours camp).

It is essential that all volunteers be at the following rendezvous. At 12 noon you will proceed to hike along the ABERGWESYN road towards Cwm Irfon. You will be picked up along this road. Special pick-up drivers will approach you in cars and will ask you the way to Abbey Cwm Hir. Your reply shall be — "Llewelyn rest in peace."

Above all else remember the following points. 1) Do not arouse suspicions or draw attention to yourself. 2) Do not talk to strangers. 3) Watch out for Special Branch. 4) Do not travel in big groups, or collect in a group upon seeing others you may know. 5) Do not recognise others at any time during the day until you are picked up.

Provisional Army Council,
Free Wales Army.

J.C.Evans, C. in C., FWA.
Llanbedrpontsteffan,   Ceredigion.

READ THIS — MEMORISE AND DESTROY!

*   *   *

From the small town of Tregaron in the county of Dyfed, an ancient drovers' road winds over the southern Cambrian Mountains to emerge at Llanwrtyd Wells. The road traverses some of the wildest and emptiest country in the British Isles with only the tiny settlement of Abergwesyn to remind the stranger that he is still in an inhabited country, and not an endless desolation of bleak and barren hills. It was decided to hold a training camp in these hills at the end of August 1968 to enable the Mid and South Wales columns of the FWA to carry out combined manoeuvres. On this occasion Keith Griffiths felt impelled to join with the military wing of the nationalist movement: "The Investiture was getting closer. The Patriotic Front had been organising the anti-investiture campaign and I thought that the Army had got to contribute something to it. We were all determined to do something on the day of the ceremony, and the idea was to get people into Caernarfon by force if necessary and take direct action there. If it meant seizing buildings or even setting fire to them, so be it. But to take action, block the roads, prevent the ceremony. Now to do this meant having an organised body of men. To me the only possibility for this was the Free Wales Army. So I then became more involved with them, and helped organise the camp at Abergwesyn.

"For me personally it turned out to be a fiasco; unfortunately I again arrived late. I was hitch-hiking and my last lift was with an undercover policeman. He picked me up and he was very chatty. He turned the conversation to nationalism and began mentioning people that he knew. I sussed him out, that he was a copper. So to mislead him I asked him to drop me off further on than I was supposed to travel. So eventually he dropped me off, and then I had to start hitching back. I got to Llanwrtyd very late and saw dozens of policemen on the streets. I made my way along the river bank to the campsite, and sat there wondering

Scenes at the FWA camp at Abergwesyn

where the hell everybody was. It was empty, completely deserted. I thought no one had turned up. I slept the night in a barn, then made my way to Tregaron. There I found out what had happened… "

All the leading members of the FWA had shown up for the camp, Denis Coslett, Vivian Davies, Bonar Thomas, Tony Lewis etc. plus some sixty to seventy of their columns' volunteers. A new recruit had also tried to join them, his name was Detective Sergeant John Lavery of the Regional Crime Squad.

Cayo Evans, as chief organiser, was also there… "The original meeting for the Summer Camp was at Abergwesyn, where the Berwyn Pass comes out on the eastern side of the Cambrians. There is a barn on the side of the road and I covered this area previously on horseback and located a handy site. Keith Griffiths and myself had sent out notices to most of our uniformed members with instructions, and a rather dramatic password and answer.

"I arrived at the campsite before most of the others, driving an old lorry, on which I carried guns, ammo etc. The boys began arriving, some on foot, others in a variety of vehicles. Dai Bonar told me that he'd passed a stranger with a heavy chin stubble and carrying a huge backpack, who was wandering around as though he wasn't sure where he had to go. Eventually this unshaven stranger showed up, in a car with a whole pile of brand new camping gear in the back. I asked him the password, and he gave it. Then asked where he was from?

'Cardiff.' He told me.

'Whose column do you belong to?'

'Geth's.' (Keith Griffiths)

"At this point Vivian Davies called me on one side, and told me that the stranger was a policeman. Viv could always smell the Law a mile away. We were in the barn by this time, where I'd stashed all the guns, and the stranger was outside. He'd unpacked a brand new camping stove, which he'd had trouble in fixing together, and was busily making tea and coffee for the lads. In the barn a heated argument then developed.

"Some of our boys wanted to shoot the stranger there and then, and dispose of the body up in the hills. I wasn't against shooting any infiltrating informer, but I didn't want to see an innocent man get harmed. I questioned the fellow some more, and he had ready enough answers, so I decided to go in search of Gethin and check it out. I drove into Llanwrtyd and found the town swarming with Special Branch. I was stopped, they pulled me out of the cab and searched the lorry.

'You've really done it this time, Cayo,' one kept informing me with an air of glee. 'It's what we've been waiting for. The authorities wanted you to do this.'

'Do what? What's wrong with going camping?'

'Don't get clever with us, Cayo!'

"The stale old argument went on and on, and I kept trying to look for Gethin, but couldn't see him. Eventually they let me go and I picked up a couple more of our late arrivals and took them with me. Back at the campsite the air was thick with tension and the stranger looked scared to death. Finally he said that he would go himself and look for Gethin, so that he could give confirmation of his identity. He sped away in his car, and never reappeared until our trial. It was, of course, Lavery, the Special Branch man.

"Our position by the barn was precarious, because by now the police cars were periodically driving backwards and forwards past us to the accompaniment of cheers, jeers and catcalls. But it only needed one of them to stop and check the barn's interior, and we would have been faced with a very dangerous situation. There were an awful lot of guns in there by now, and a large amount of ammunition.

"We decided to pull out and get back into Cardiganshire, but we had also got to leave the SB's behind. I knew of an old disused bridle track past a farm called Nant Stalwyn that went over the mountains, through the forestry, and came out near the ruins of Strata Florida Abbey by Pontrydfendigaid. So off we went. We had to push some of the vehicles up the hill called Devil's Elbow, down past Nant-yr-Hwch then off the road and onto the bridle track. The ruts were terrible and several times my lorry nearly tipped, which gave me a hell of a fright each time. The police convoy came after us, a couple of SB's in each, but we weren't concerned because a little further on the track had collapsed down the hillside, leaving an abrupt dead-end.

"On the hillside above however was a forestry track. Sixty or seventy men can and did manage to manhandle our vehicles bodily up the hill and onto this other track. But it was impossible for the police to follow us, they hadn't got the manpower to heave their powerful cars up the hillside. There on the track they sat watching us, scowls like thunderclouds on all faces. We waved farewell and fired a few shots in the air as a parting gesture, and then we were away. We camped at an alternative site miles into the hills, with all our vehicles hidden deep in the forestry plantations. Which was just as well, because later a police helicopter came buzzing around looking for us... Since we now couldn't do our training in the daylight; we did night firing and movement exercises instead, all good and necessary experience for our lads... and after the two days elapsed went back to our homes... "

*   *   *

Although the police had been discomfited at

Abergwesyn, the month of August brought them one major success. Owain Williams the bail jumping nationalist was arrested at Birmingham Airport on the 27th day of that month...

"I'd jumped bail early in 1968 and about six months later I was in Ireland, and I'd met a girl named Katherine. I was by then living in a tent on the beach at Kinsale in County Cork, and was desperately short of money. Katherine would get me food from the restaurant where she worked as a waitress. My tent was very easy to recognise, it had lots of roasted chicken bones outside it. My beard was ginger and my hair was black, and Kinsale was full of rich yachtsmen who were convinced that I'd dyed either one or the other growth. Every time I went to see my girl she'd say, 'Och, you disperate lookin' character!'

"My cover at that time was that I was a Rhodesian who because UDI had been declared couldn't go back to Rhodesia. One night Katherine insisted that I shave my beard off. Full of wine, I forgot that I was going back to England in two days, and shaved the beard.

"Katherine and myself flew back from Cork to Birmingham, we had one little suitcase between us. Two toothbrushes, one tube of toothpaste, pyjamas, towel, bar of soap and a newspaper.

"While I was at the customs counter I saw these two shifty looking characters edging up to me, wearing macs, hats pulled down over their eyes, and hands dug very deep into their mac pockets. The customs man took ages to check our suitcase, and remarked.

'You haven't got much luggage, have you.'

'No,' says Katherine. 'We're travelling light. We're just going to a conference.'

"I picked up the suitcase and as we passed, this one man in a pulled down hat tapped me on the shoulder... 'Yes, you're having a conference with us.' He told me. 'Mr Williams isn't it?'

'Yes.'

'Owain Williams?'

'Yes.'

'Come with us, please.' And he stuck something through his coat into my ribs. Katherine turned to me and exclaimed.

'Jesus, Joseph and Mary! What have ye done?'

"I had a little notebook with addresses written in it, which I managed to slip to her to hide under her clothes. They arrested both of us, and kept us in Birmingham for two nights. For the first day without food, perhaps a softening up process. Then the Caernarfon police said they were coming for me, and not to let anybody see me.

"The policemen from Caernarfon arrived and in front of me demanded very authoritatively, 'Has he talked yet?' — as though I were a speaking budgie or something similar.

"Katherine was released and phoned my mother to let her know I'd been arrested, then they took me in a convoy of three cars, two men in each, with me in the middle one. In the car one said to me:

'So you've come back to give yourself up?'

'No, I've just come back.'

'Well, you've come back to face what's coming to you, have you?'

"I thought it was strange to keep asking me this question, but only replied, 'No, I've just come back.'

"Later in court the policeman said that they'd cautioned me and I'd replied, 'Ohh yes, I've come back to face what is coming to me.' As though after six months on the run I'd come back and say that?

"After another nearly three months' solitary confinement in Risley Remand centre my case came up. Funny enough my case started on Guy Fawkes day, which was apt for an explosives case. It lasted four or five days; I was in the dock myself for two or three of them. I told them that I'd gone on the run to prepare my defence because I'd been framed by the police, and I'd needed time for that preparation. This was debatable of course, but they couldn't prove otherwise… "

Owain Williams was charged with having unlawfully in his possession on or about November 3rd 1967, 13 sticks of gelignite. One prosecution witness, John Gwilym Jones, aged 20, gave dramatic testimony of taking the Free Wales Army oath while Williams was present and having a knife pressed to his throat while he did so. The witness talked of raids planned on British Army armouries, of uprisings to take Caernarfon town, and of a marksman who was going to put a shot through Mr Cledwyn Hughes' car windscreen to frighten him; and talked a great deal about delivering and accepting sticks of gelignite.

This testimony notwithstanding the jury found Owain Williams 'Not guilty', and he walked from the court to the cheers of the many nationalist supporters who had packed the courtroom each day of the trial. Owain Williams had a further brush with the police while leaving the court…

"When Detective Sergeant Glyn Owens had first arrested me in January 1968, he told me, 'Well, at the end of all this we can shake hands and say the better man won.'

"As I left the court with my solicitor and barrister, we went out the back way to avoid the crowds at the front. I passed Glyn Owens and his mate. I couldn't resist holding out my hand and saying.

'Shake hands?'

'He made no reply, and I said. 'Oh come on now, you said that after this you'd shake and say the better man won. Well he did … '

"Fair play to Owens, he did shake hands, but as I went on his mate growled, 'We'll get you again, you bastard!'"

The Free Wales Army had inevitably made their presence felt at the trial. When the judge's Bentley limousine drew up outside the court, a very ancient Rolls Royce flying a Red Dragon pennant drew up in front of it, and out jumped a group of FWA men in oddly assorted uniforms. The crowd cheered and an onlooker said later, "It didn't look as if the police knew who to salute first, the judge, or the boys."

After the case, and indicative of public interest in it, there was a press conference held in a Caernarfon hotel at which over a hundred journalists were present. Once more it appeared that nationalism was winning the publicity war… But in the September of 1968 something had occurred which for once was bad publicity for the nationalist cause. An airman had been injured by a bomb.

Chapter Twenty Four

UP TO SEPTEMBER 1968 the only adverse publicity, from their own view point, that the Free Wales Army had received was because of Denis Coslett's much-loved dog, Gelert. For the benefit of Mr Elfyn Thomas, a reporter from the *Herald of Wales*, Denis had fitted a harness to the highly-trained dog's back with pockets in it into which sticks of gelignite could be inserted. He told the reporter that the dog was now a mobile missile, and that he had another twenty such dogs hidden at a farmhouse up in the mountains. Coslett claimed that the dogs, all large and powerful Alsatians, were trained to carry magnetic mines strapped to their backs and on the word of command, 'Attack!' to run beneath tanks, armoured cars, trucks etc. The magnetic mine would stick to the target vehicle, and both dog and target would be blown to smithereens.

The article was duly published describing these 'Kamikaze' dogs; and Denis Coslett was inundated with hundreds of abusive letters from dog-lovers all over the world berating him for his vile cruelty. "You cruel bastard!" was one of the milder expletives showered upon him. This crazy-sounding idea was in fact feasible, having been used successfully on the Russian Front during World War Two. Though, in truth, Denis Coslett had no plans to use his beloved Gelert on such a mission, and the dogs in the mountains never existed.

On the run up to September 1968, the FWA publicity machine was rolling along in top gear. An Israeli television producer, Gideon Haendler, had made a documentary film about the FWA shot mostly in the Black Mountains near Pontaber, and lavishly endowed with scenes of explosions and guerrilla ambushes etc. Gideon Haendler was to claim in early January 1969 that policemen led by Commander Jock Wilson visited his cutting room near Covent Garden on January 2nd and demanded to see the film. After he had shown them an eighth of the four hour film they asked to see the rest, and when he refused threatened to confiscate it. He also alleged that the police wanted to stop him selling the film to television companies. A spokesman at Scotland Yard said on the night of January 2nd, "The police are making no comment on this matter."

The *Daily Telegraph* colour supplement had during July 1968 also photographed and prepared a major article on the FWA to be published on September 6th. As had a Swedish journalist, Kurt Malardstedt for a full-colour page in the *Dagens Nyheter*, Stockholm's leading newspaper to be published on September 28th.

Then, on Monday September 9th in the number Two control tower of the Royal Air Force practice range on Cefn Sands, Pembrey, overlooking Camarthen Bay, Warrant Officer William Hougham, a married man aged 42, picked up a cardboard shoe box. The box exploded in his hands causing him severe injuries.

Commander Jock Wilson of the Special branch immediatelyheaded the search for the bombers, and his teams of detectives flooded the area. The FWA leaders and other nationalists were as a matter of course brought in for questioning within hours, but denied all knowledge of this particular explosion. There were indeed some very puzzling aspects to this incident. Both the FWA active service units, and the MAC cells had always been expressly ordered that no bomb should ever be placed without extreme precautions to avoid human injuries. Many missions had been aborted precisely because there was a chance of human injury occurring, if only a slight one. Also, if any planted bomb failed to explode after an allotted time of two hours a warning must always be phoned in anonymously to the police giving the bomb's location. No official FWA or MAC operation had been planned to hit this particular target; and each FWA commandant could only initially assume that one of their fellows had instigated this Pembrey action on the spur of the moment, for some reason as yet unknown to the Army.

The injured RAF man enabled the politicians to condemn the unknown bombers with for once, moral justification, and even among the extremist groups there was angry criticism and condemnation of the action. Because the last thing that any of the independence movements' leaders wanted, was to place a potent ready-made propaganda weapon into the hands of their opponents; and this is precisely what the Pembrey explosion had done.

The incident also led to an exchange between Cayo Evans and Commander Jock Wilson which was to have far-reaching consequences, and later during the trial lead to many charges, counter-charges and denials by barristers and witnesses. Here, Cayo Evans gives his account of what occurred after the Pembrey bomb.

"That summer, 1968, came the trump card the Special Branch had waited for: the Pembrey explosion. This occurred in an RAF camp in Carmarthenshire. A disgruntled RAF man made a bomb trap to get some officer he didn't like, and the bomb was disturbed by a Warrant Officer Houghman who subsequently lost an eye and a finger. It was put over the news that he had been very badly injured by an FWA bomb, and that his death was imminent. Large numbers of our members were arrested and taken to the police HQ at

Carmarthen. Now at the time I had no idea who had set the bomb, and thought it was probably one of the Southern units of the FWA.

"I was arrested and taken to Carmarthen, and interrogated all night by different teams of policemen, then by Jock Wilson. Since we had previously made threats against military installations in Wales, and claimed responsibility for the previous explosions, it looked bad for us. Threats were made, all sorts of questions were asked. They said to me,

'We're holding you now until the man dies, then we'll charge you with conspiracy to murder. I'll see to it you get 15 years.'

'That man is dying fast, you really are in a mess!'

'It's the rope for you, this time.'

"Thus Jock Wilson's drift went along, switching from threats to sympathetic agreement, from the bombs to the arms we had. But there was not much to be gained from my interrogation that had not already been printed in the newspapers. A high-ranking detective named Vaughan took over the cross-examination, a very skilful interrogator. I wanted to shift the line of questioning off the bombs, and as he was interested in our arms I steered the talk that way. Then he offered,

'Things have got out of control, the guns may get into the wrong hands. You hand them over, and we'll drop all this.'

"This seemed better than doing 15 years, so I answered to the effect that I agreed with this course of action. He fetched Jock Wilson and I was taken into another room. It was then that I made the arms deal with Jock Wilson.

"The deal I made was that I would dump the arms that I had access to, in some secluded spot. I was to phone the Police HQ when I had done this and ask for Jock Wilson. I was to use the name Arthur, and tell him exactly where the guns were, giving a map reference so that they could be picked up. In exchange for this I would now be unconditionally released, and none of our men would be prosecuted. Great emphasis was made on the secrecy of this deal. During our trial the following summer the judge went to great lengths to prevent details of this bargain becoming known.

"The following day I went to the farm where the arms were concealed in a large metal box, and to another hide where the ammunition was kept. I put the lot in a sack, keeping back a small silver-plated -22 revolver for self-protection. I drove north across the Tregaron bog to where I knew of a lake called Maes-Llyn. I hid the car, crossed the disused railway, dismantled the guns as best I could and hurled them and the ammunition into the lake. I then went to Llanddewi Brefi where I phoned through as agreed and gave Wilson the details… "

The next day police frogmen found the arms, and the newspapers headlined the story, complete with photographs of frogmen surfacing triumphantly with arms and ammunition: Lugers, stenguns, Mauser machine pistols. Detective Supt. Vivian Fisher told reporters that both arms and ammunition were found after an anonymous phone tip-off. Later, during the FWA men's trial, Mr John Gower QC, defending David Bonar Thomas, was to cross-examine Jock Wilson about the alleged arms deal. The policeman denied any pact had been made, and the judge told the jury to disregard any reference to it, saying that the allegation had been 'truthfully denied' by the policeman.

*   *   *

After the Pembrey bomb all pretence of any amicable

exchanges between extremists and policemen disappeared. The Special Branch hardened its tactics; and Cayo Evans maintains that attempts at bribery were also made…

"During the latter part of 1968 we were constantly harrassed by the police. Our homes were searched on numerous occasions, our phones were tapped and our mail was censored. This could work at times to our advantage. If we wanted to cause a scare or feed them (the police) with useless information it was only necessary to phone one of the boys, or write him a letter. My own phone was laboriously joined to a tape-recorder in the Plas Crug building in Aberystwyth (the government building). There was, and perhaps still is, a special room there where the phones of all local extremists were hitched to tape recorders.

"There were also attempts made to bribe different FWA commandants to give information. I remember on one occasion Det. Sgt. Walford-Davies and another Special Branch man came to my home. We had the usual by now stereotyped argument to begin with.

"Policeman/ 'We have nothing against your aims, but we condemn your methods. Make no mistake, we will catch these men; and even if they're not your pals, you do know who they are.'

"Myself/ 'All I know is it's not me. I am merely the spokesman for the organisation, etc… etc… '

"Towards the end of this particular conversation, Walford-Davies said, 'Look here, I have instructions from high-up. We are prepared to give you a suitcase containing £50,000 in used banknotes, if you give us the names we want.'

'Bring it along by all means,' I told him, 'and you can watch me burn the bloody lot.'

"Needless to say, we didn't part amicably following this interview … "

Another interview between Cayo Evans and the police which again did not end on a congenial note took place at the by-now annual Cilmeri Rally, which on this occasion was held on Saturday December 14th 1968... " We met up prior to the rally in a small pub close to the Cilmeri Stone, named appropriately the *Prince Llewelyn*. As I went in I spotted a Special Branch man sitting amongst the boys. They were always fairly easy to pick out, their dress-fashion then being a Gannex raincoat, Hush Puppy shoes and a Robin Hood hat. I let it be clearly known that he was Special Branch, and he left the pub.

"That night, after the ceremony at the Stone we held a torchlight procession through Builth Wells. As usual the town was fairly full with Special Branch, and several of our boys were shoved around by them. Gethin (Keith Griffiths) got into an argument and was hit and kicked by one of the police in the scuffle. I came out of a public house and a local plain-clothes man, Tom Davies, started to call out abuse. I knew him because at a previous rally in Machynlleth he had tried to infiltrate us, claiming he was a tool machine operator. I went down to him and some words were exchanged. Instantly uniformed police piled out of an alley and sealed the street off, while two more plain-clothes men joined Davies and the three of them jumped at me and began giving me a beating.

"I was frog-marched to the police station where a more scientific hammering was administered, both my arms being twisted up my back so that I was bent double with my feet off the ground and my head down, while they banged at my kidneys, back and ribs, and I took a boot in my face.

"A police Inspector by the name of Murphy arrived and they stopped hammering me and stuck me in a chair. They then charged me with assaulting the police! Three detectives without a mark on them, and me bleeding! The Inspector told me to wash the blood off, then allowed Tony Lewis inside to see me. Because by now there was a large crowd outside and things were looking ugly, flaming torches and stones being hurled at the police station. The police wanted me to sign the bail form and release me. But I refused. 'You've abducted me and beaten me up, so how long can you hold me?' I asked.

"The local inspector then arrived, also various reinforcements, but our crowd had them outnumbered; clods of earth and stones were coming through the windows and there was a lot of shouting and scuffling going on outside. I was ushered out of a side door and into a waiting police car. They were taking me to another station at Llandrindod Wells. As we pulled up there I made a jump for it and legged it up the road with the posse in hot pursuit. The chase ended when I was rugger tackled, brought down then led to the station and put in a cell for the night.

"The duty policeman was a decent type and early in the morning let me out to sit and chat with him by the fireside, and drink tea. Later I signed the bail form and was released. I went and had a photo taken of my facial injuries, and from a doctor got a medical report about my body bruises and abrasions. But when I came up before the magistrates in January these were not allowed as evidence. I considered that the police were proven liars during the case, and expected to win it. However the magistrates had received a phonecall from the Home Office with instructions to convict me, and I was judged guilty… "

Cayo Evans was sentenced to four months imprisonment, suspended for two years, on a charge of assaulting a detective.

Keith Griffiths has his own memories of Builth Wells…

"My recollection of Builth Wells is this. Castro (a friend) and I were walking down the street, and we were taken aside by the police. Fisher was there, the head of the police in West Wales, but I'm not sure if John Owens (another high-ranking policeman) was there. The police held me over the bonnet of a car and threatened me, and they were talking to Castro. Castro said something to one of the police, and the copper kneed him in the groin, and Castro crumpled up. They were warning us to get out of Builth Wells. Lots of the police there were Cockneys, Londoners in plain-clothes. Anyway, we went back to the pub and told the others. Cayo was taken in at that point. We marched on the police station with flaming torches and stones were thrown. Fisher came out and ranted at us, followed by the rest of the police, and there was some scuffling, but in the end we had to run for it. There was a German or Swedish television crew there who made a film of it all… "

Not only had the authorities' attitude hardened against the Patriotic Front and the FWA but luck was also running out for them in other ways. Crossgates, the scene of a failed operation, was to prove a jinx once again when one of the Swansea columns attempted a second attack on the aqueduct…

"Our failure at Crossgates nagged at me like a toothache. I couldn't put it out of my mind. So eventually it was decided that my column would try again to knock it out. We did face more problems this time because of the dossiers the police had built up on our lads, and also the increased security measures covering all pipelines. Any nationalist by that time was likely to be stopped, searched and questioned by wandering Special Branch, so the difficulty first of all was to get the geli to the target.

"Myself and another bloke dressed up very conservatively and took a suitcase each with us by train from Swansea to Llandrindod Wells. We travelled separately with the geli in one case and the timing switch, batteries, wire,

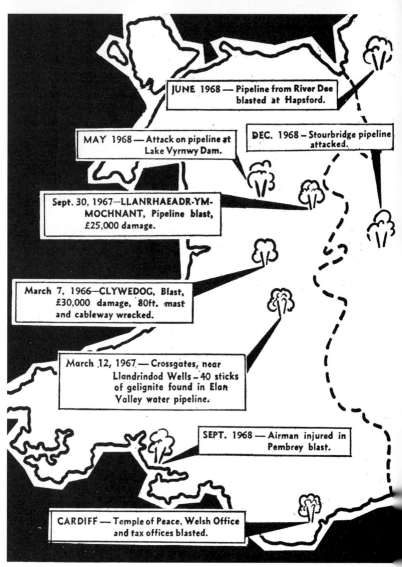

JUNE 1968 — Pipeline from River Dee blasted at Hapsford.

MAY 1968 — Attack on pipeline at Lake Vyrnwy Dam.

DEC. 1968 – Stourbridge pipeline attacked.

Sept. 30, 1967—LLANRHAEADR-YM-MOCHNANT, Pipeline blast, £25,000 damage.

March 7, 1966—CLYWEDOG, Blast, £30,000 damage, 80ft. mast and cableway wrecked.

March 12, 1967 — Crossgates, near Llandrindod Wells – 40 sticks of gelignite found in Elan Valley water pipeline.

SEPT. 1968 — Airman injured in Pembrey blast.

CARDIFF — Temple of Peace, Welsh Office and tax offices blasted.

A Western Mail *map showing the bombing campaign up to December 1968*

216

etc. in the other. The actual assault team of three men were to meet us in Llandrindod, take the stuff from there by van to the target and deal with it. We had our usual trouble over lack of transport; you must remember that we were all working men with very little in the way of cash funds. One of the assault team owned an old van, which normally was covered with nationalist stickers and flags. It was the only vehicle we could get hold of, so we were forced to use it. The lad stripped all the stickers off, hoping to make it less noticeable. I'm afraid it had just the opposite effect, because the local detectives straight away were asking him why he'd taken the stuff off. Had he finished with nationalism or what? But there was no help for it, we had no alternative transport, so we went ahead.

"The three-man assault team started off by road, and on the way were stopped three times by different squad cars, and the van was searched each time. One of the police actually said to the boys that he knew they were going off on one of their bloody nationalist capers. Naturally by the time Llandrindod was reached the three lads' nerve had gone, and they were convinced that the job had already been grassed. The van owner wouldn't take the geli from us, and insisted we abort the mission. I couldn't find it in my own heart to condemn him for that, but on the other hand we couldn't risk travelling back by train with the stuff. It was a safe bet the law would be waiting for us at the other end. So we threw the stuff into the river at Pontardulais. I felt bloody sick about it, I'll tell you. Bloody sick!"

Chapter Twenty Five

THE FWA MAY WELL have been rendered almost impotent at this time by police activity, but the Mudiad Amddiffyn Cymru had most definitely not. Earlier that year, 1968, the Corps of Drums of the Wrexham T.A. had been wound up because of lack of funds. Upon this happening John Jenkins, Alders and others had taken over the responsibility for the local Army Cadet band. Jenkins' motives for this move were admittedly double-edged. He had a deeply sincere love for military music and pageantry, and greatly enjoyed training youngsters in these skills. But also...

"While in the Corps of Drums, and later the Army Cadet Band, I had additional excuses for moving around. As I said before, our cell system was a good one, but it depended on one thing. My mobility. My ability to move around from place to place, to obtain equipment, to reconnoitre targets, to contact my cell officers. The only way to cope with any unexpected demand was always to carry a load of stuff with me as I moved around. It's very worrying mind, taking the wife and kids down to South Wales for a family weekend, sitting on top of 60lbs of explosive beneath the seat. I'm a fairly cool person, but it does tend to affect the nerves; and contrary to what people say, one doesn't get used to it. It's not a thing that one shrugs off as it comes along. I didn't enjoy doing such things, it always used to affect me physically. Here am I, the steel man, the iron man, the concrete man, and all the other bloody things they later called me, but the point was that always before I went on any job I inevitably had the runs. I'm no man of tremendous courage, or anything like that. That's not the way it works. The way it works is, that you consider what you are going to have to do, and you consider the alternative if you don't do it, and so you do it, basically because of the motivation. You know you are doing the right thing for your cause, and the fact also that you know that if you don't do it, then no one else will. So you have to do it.

"Anyway, I was now well placed to move around, because my army job was in charge of the dental stores at Saighton Camp, the Chester army HQ. Which gave me the use of a very large building, to which only I had the keys; and access to all the stores and machinery which only I controlled. So I was able to store my gelignite and construct my bombs there with complete safety. Also I was the senior NCO in my regiment in Western Command; there was just the colonel and myself. So it was my job to dodge around the various units in the Command checking stores, holding inspections etc. Therefore it was quite in order for me to be moving around Wales. The cadets band then was both a pleasure and an added excuse. Since you must never go anywhere solely to meet someone, you must always go for some not ostensible purpose, but for a genuine purpose, and then you slide the covert meeting in between, or during or afterwards etc. So if anybody should question what you were doing in a place you can reply… I was with the Cadet band… I was checking the stores at such and such a camp… or similar. Then if the questioner should check your story he finds of course that you were doing just that.

"For example, the Liverpool Waterworks were holding an exhibition of their works and how they operated which I wanted to see. The exhibition was carefully monitored because of the pipeline explosions. The cadets went up there to give a show, so during the break Alders and I were able to wander into the Waterworks show and study it very carefully without arousing suspicion. We were there after all for a genuine reason, we had the band... "

Running the cadets band brought an unexpected bonus to John Jenkins' organisation. The cadet force possessed like many other cadet forces, a very large selection of old maps and documents. Any map printed before 1950 had the lines of the main water pipelines marked on them by a series of small dots. Maps after this date did not. At ground level it was possible to follow the map and trace the pipes until they emerged from the ground. Easier said than actually done, but pipes must always eventually emerge above railway lines, rivers etc. Jenkins passed some maps onto his cell officers, and one of them made good use of the documents...

"I wanted to knock out one of the main Midland pipes, and when the MAC commander passed this map onto me, I found that the line of one of the Birmingham Corporation pipes passed right through my area. I followed the map for miles, and must have covered sixty of those, right into England, before I found a place which I could hit. I activated my cell after I'd been to the spot a few times to check it out, and we took it in turns to keep an eye on the target. The main snag for us was that the police had been keeping this site under twenty-four hour watch. It was at a place called West Hagley close to Stourbridge in Worcestershire. We were lucky though, because just after we'd made up our minds to strike, they stopped the twenty-four hour watch, and only came every two hours to have a look,

"The pipes, two or three big ones, came out to pass over a railway cutting, and the police would drive up this lane to them, have a quick look around, and then drive away. The other problem for us was that the railway line was the main one from the Midlands to South Wales, and there were trains up and down every few minutes. We were under very strict orders that no harm must come to any train. I was forgetting another snag, there was also a cottage about thirty yards away.

"On the last day of November 1968, I went with my number two man to do a final checkout. We found some high ground from where we could overlook everything, and plan our line of approach. But we noticed there were still a lot of people floating around near there. I knew there was a bridge about a mile to one side of the pipes, so as soon as it got dark we shoved the car in a car park on a main road where there were a lot of other cars and it wouldn't attract any attention, and went to the bridge. We went over it and down along the railway line to do our last checks.

"On the night of the 1st December, we followed the same routine, except that this time we had the bomb with us. I was carrying it strapped to my back, and I was ill at the time. I'd got a bad dose of the flu, and to be honest I'd sooner have been at home in my bed, rather than running around with dynamite strapped to me. I couldn't even set the bomb myself, I was shivering too much, and my hands were too shaky. So I had to tell my number two what to do. He managed okay and set it so that it would do the maximum damage without bothering the cottage across the way, and without interfering with the trains. That was really dicey because when we'd checked the passenger timetables, we'd found that freight trains used the line a lot as well. It's always very hard to find out the times of the freights because they don't mention them on timetables. That's how I caught the bloody flu, I spent three whole nights there keeping note of the times the freights passed our target spot. It was the best I could do, and I'd found that there was about a three minute gap to aim for. Well, we managed it pretty well smack on. The pipe blew without breaking a single window in the cottage, although afterwards they said the blast was heard nine miles away; and without any danger to the trains. The police had just left the spot when we went to it, so we knew that we had two clear hours to work in, and could take care to get it just right... I felt really chuffed when I read about it afterwards, really great. I felt I'd shown our High Command that I could tackle any job they wanted to give me, even Buckingham Palace... "

No one was ever charged with this bombing.

Det. Chief. Supt. Robert Booth of the West Mercian Constabulary opined that Welsh Nationalists, "a lunatic element from the English-Welsh border", had been responsible for the "dastardly attack".

Dr Gareth Morgan Jones, Plaid Cymru's assistant general secretary said the policeman's remarks were outrageous and a "political assassination of the Welsh Nationalist movement."

The shattered pipeline made no accusation, or rebuttal, it merely gushed water, lots and lots of water...

The aftermath of the West Hagley bomb

Chapter Twenty Six

INVESTITURE YEAR, 1969, had come, and during the cold January days it appeared that up to this point the Welsh extremists had had things all their own way. Even on the rare occasions that legal action had been brought against them, the defendant extremists were either acquitted, or given farcically light penalties. It was openly said by many people in British political and security circles, that in their anxiety to prevent the creation of nationalist martyrs the authorities had been over lenient. In extremist circles there was an ever-growing feeling of strength and confidence, given impetus by the continued and absolute failure of the police to track down the bombers.

The irrepressible Denis Coslett had even invited Prime Minister Harold Wilson to meet him in the middle of the River Tywi for peace talks. Denis Coslett to sit in one coracle, and Harold Wilson in another. Perhaps mindful of the failure of the Rhodesian peace talks aboard HMS Tiger, there was no acceptance of this Welsh offer by the Prime Minister.

On a more serious note there was a strong determination among the leaders of the FWA and the political Patriotic Front to carry out some really spectacular action on Investiture Day itself, July 1st 1969.

Denis Coslett had made his own independent plan, together with Vivian Davies… "What we planned on doing was to drive into Cardiff on Investiture day, in a hired bus. About a dozen of us from my own and Viv's columns. Once there we would burst into the Welsh Office, that omnipotent

The "irresistable" Denis Coslett in the full FWA outfit

building that George Thomas occupied, and occupy it ourselves for six or seven days, using arms to hold off any attempt at recapture. We'd obviously lose the battle, but because the Government security measures would all be centred on Caernarfon for the investiture, it would have been easy for us to take and hold the Welsh Office for a time… "

Cayo Evans and Keith Griffiths had other ideas, even more ambitious ones. Keith Griffiths wrote:

"Annwyl Cayo,

The plans are fixed for Caernarfon we risel

The AICC (Anti-investiture committee) will be organising the final events. Non-violent.

1) Sat. June 28th. Assembly of supporters in Snowdonia at camps.

2) Sunday June 29th. Raising the Flag Rally on Snowdon Peak.

3) Monday June 30th. March to Caernarfon Castle with Rally.

4) Tuesday July 1st. Demonstration.

It's up to the FWA and PF to take the lead and if stopped on the way to Caernarfon we smash our way thru or infiltrate into the town and by Tuesday morning we must occupy as much of the town as possible.

So Cayo — it all rests with you whether the 'Byddire is organised, equipped and prepared for this. The Front will be. Will the FWA?

We march and take Caernarfon at all costs. Arm ourselves with shotguns, guns, bows slings, pikes, weapons of all sorts.

First aid stations will be arranged!

We must take Caernarfon! So for God sake get the Byddin organised.

We fight our way into the town, the Investiture must be stopped!"

*   *   *

Later the plans were to become more detailed. In another document sent to Cayo Evans, his colleague of the Patriotic Front was more explicit…

"Specially trained and equipped volunteers of Cilmeriad squads will be active throughout the battle.

> These will be responsible for special services and will lead the attack on the castle and other key positions in the town held by the enemy; and also the task of assassinating the Pretender if necessary, and other key people on the black list."

Cayo Evans himself was equally determined to stop the Investiture. He was to reply:

> "With regard to the 'I'. OK you know the scheme. I am going ahead with it somehow.
>
> If we have sufficient men we can form a relief column. The main group will be in the camp. If you can come up some weekend I will take you up there.
>
> Every man must carry a pack of provisions for three weeks. Water bottle, sleeping bag — they must get shotguns, single-barrel Spanish or Russian are only about £10.
>
> I will have a certain amount of the automatic stuff, but not sufficient for everyone.
>
> Up until now all work has been done independently by the columns. We must now combine the fighting force. I will be honest, most of my boys are scattered about. If I run short I am calling in the IRA.
>
> They have offered all assistance, and their boys are well-trained and well-armed… "

Although at first glance these plans seemed to some of the FWA members to be preposterous, the sheer heady excitement generated by such ideas took hold of their imaginations. An old scout-car abandoned after the war in a remote Northern farmstead was discovered, and mechanics from the Northern columns of the FWA began to renovate it, reasoning that at Caernarfon on the day it would undoubtedly be the most powerful weapon immediately available to either side. Light wooden rafts were experimented with, the idea being to strap rows of smoke bombs to them and send them floating through the town's sewers, creating smoke-screens and confusion all through the streets. An Irish sympathiser owned an Auster plane, which he kept in Ireland. He offered this to the FWA, and they eagerly accepted. If the IRA could use helicopters to drop milk-churns full of explosives onto police stations, why couldn't the FWA emulate them using the Auster. For both FWA commandants and Patriotic Front leaders all other activities became subordinate and one objective only became of paramount importance. The plan for Investiture Day… Unfortunately for that plan, the police struck first…

*　　*　　*

The police strike first and arrest FWA commandants

The Special Branch were well aware of the problems confronting them concerning the investiture. The event had indeed, from the point of view of the man in the street, become a polariser of opinion. But a polariser of opinion as to who would prove the stronger, the extremists, or the authorities. The one side determined to prevent the ceremony from taking place, the other side equally determined that they should stage it.

Despite the expertise and experience of policemen like Jock Wilson, Vivian Fisher and John Parkman, and the intensive and laborious work of their men, no one had been charged and convicted of bombing offences since 1963. The public, unaware of the peculiar difficulties facing investigators in the notoriously clannish and tight-knit Welsh-speaking communities were openly doubting the abilities of the police. Politicians were clamouring for action against the Welsh bombers, and the FWA by its extremely skilful exploitation of the world's media was causing grave embarrassment to the authorities.

It was through the publicity constantly given to them that a case of sorts had eventually been enabled to be built up against the various commandants of the FWA. After high-level consultation the police were given the go-ahead, and at 6 a.m. on the morning of February 26th 1969, they moved into action. The homes of the nine leading FWA and Patriotic Front members were raided by large squads of police and Special Branch, and arrests followed.

Cayo Evans, 30 years of age, Denis Coslett, 29. William Vernon Griffiths, 35. Vivian George Davies, 27. David Bonar Thomas, 46. Keith Griffiths, 22. David John Underhill, 29. Antony Harold Lewis, 31 and Dafydd Glyn Rowlands, 31. They came from all parts of Wales, and their backgrounds were as diverse as their professions. Horse breeder, miner, farmer, metal merchant, plumber, bus driver, forester, labourers. Amid harrowing scenes of crying, frightened children, distressed wives and parents, the men were handcuffed and bundled into squad cars, and later charged with various offences under the Public Order Act. From that date until their trial they were kept in solitary confinement, wearing the yellow patches and subjected to the restrictions of escapees; and harrassed by certain jailers as if they were the most ruthless of mass-murderers. Instead of men, who in the opinions of a great many people, were Welsh patriots who had served the country they loved in the way they conceived was best for Wales.

Their trial beginning in May was to last for 53 days and span three months, and apart from David John Underhill, who was quickly acquitted and released on May 28th 1969, the remainder of the defendants would not know their eventual fates until July 1st 1969, when they were to receive their sentences on the very day of the investiture they had so passionately desired to prevent. With one exception the accused men remained unyielding in their principles. The exception, William Vernon Griffiths, once so ready to be photographed holding guns beneath Dragon banners, glaring defiance and hatred of the Saxon oppressor, claimed in evidence that when he had joined the FWA he had thought it to be an organisation similar to the Salvation Army or St. John Ambulance Brigade, and that he had quit the organisation when he saw they had guns.

On June 30th 1969 the trial came to its close. David Bonar Thomas and Glyn Rowlands were judged not guilty on all charges and were released. On the 1st of July the remaining six men were sentenced.

Cayo Evans, 15 months imprisonment on each of ten charges all to run concurrently. Denis Coslett, 15 months imprisonment on each of eight charges, all to run concurrently. Keith Griffiths, 9 months imprisonment on one charge. Antony Harold Lewis, 8 months imprisonment on one charge, suspended for three years. Vivian George Davies, 6 months imprisonment on one charge, suspended for two years. William Vernon Griffiths, 3 months imprisonment on one charge suspended for two years: this was for unauthorised possession of a stengun, not normally issued to soldiers of the Salvation Army.

All through the trial the court gallery had been packed with relatives and sympathisers of the accused. The singing of the Welsh national anthem had been a frequent occurrence, and the constant shouts of encouragement to the men in the dock, and jeering of police witnesses had given an indication of the strength of feeling aroused by the case.

It could be said with justification that no man in the dock is able to retain his dignity as a human being unimpaired. Before he received his sentence, Denis Coslett, speaking on behalf of himself and his friends, restored whatever dignity, if any, had been lost by the men on trial. Standing rigidly to attention before the judge, he spoke the following words, in Welsh…

"Judge, it is right that I should address you on 'Thou' terms. I have respect for a person older than myself, but I have no respect for the symbol on the wall behind you.

"I have been brought here on charges of displaying arms, and of using physical force to promote a political object. Those at least are some of the charges against us. During the last few months you have heard very much, day after day in this case, mention of the word, 'violence'. I was for some time in the English Army, and during that time I received instruction on how to use arms and to promote violence. Therefore, I am of the opinion that that was to promote an English political object, and so was an honourable thing. There are to be seen along the length and breadth of Wales many military camps, bombing schools, rocket stations; and during the Investiture warships will be seen in the Menai Straits, and battalions of armed soldiers on the streets of Caernarfon, and in order to safeguard our English identity there will be military planes over Eryri (Snowdonia) and all this will be legal. Be not afraid, they are only to promote an English political object.

"Of course, to instruct children from the schools of Wales, namely the cadets, and to dress them in military uniform, and to instruct and train them in a military manner is no offence whatsoever... I wonder?

"English violence is right and legal, and honourable, but Welsh violence is a terrible crime. That I believe is the beginning and end of this whole show of a case.

"I shall never forget Wales in my lonely cell, and my last prayer shall be, May the God of all Freedom strengthen Wales to cast off Her fetters. Tonight I shall sleep in a lonely cell, and tomorrow I shall wear prison uniform, but for me it will be a far more honourable uniform than the costliest dress of the slave and the serf. It is only the serf and the coward who believes that the suffering and inhumanity of prison life is shame upon man. I do not believe that it is possible to kill the soul that has been inspired by the spirit of freedom. The only arm I shall now use, is the pen. I will not ask you for forgiveness as did the Protestant leader, Ian Paisley; I seek no favours from any man in the world. I sought to serve Wales, and now I am prepared to suffer for Wales... I am ready for your sentence... Free Wales!"

The courtroom erupted with cheering at the conclusion of Coslett's words, and unable to restore order, Mr Justice Thompson caused the public galleries to be cleared. Only Denis Coslett's wife, sobbing bitterly, was allowed to remain.

The arrest and imprisonment of its leading commandants, coupled with the ongoing intensive security operations still being carried out by the police and Special Branch dealt the FWA a blow from which it could not recover. The organisation, once so full of ardour, fell apart. The Free Wales Army, to all intents and purposes, was a spent force.

But the police had still got to defeat the Mudiad Amddiffyn Cymru...

Chapter Twenty Seven

WITH THE FWA COMMANDANTS in custody and their trial due to begin on April 16th 1969, the police could be forgiven for feeling that they had broken the back of violent extremism in Wales. As Commander Jock Wilson told Cayo Evans after his arrest:

"There'll be no more explosions now, Cayo. We've put a stop to your gallop."

The Commander was back at Scotland Yard when at 2.11 a.m. in the morning of Thursday, April 10th 1968, the offices of the Inland Revenue, part of the six-storied Hamilton House in the heart of Chester town centre's re-development area, were blasted by a bomb. More than two hundred windows in the building were shattered, a gaping hole torn through a six inch reinforced concrete wall, windows broken up to half a mile away; and thousands of tax documents sent floating across the city. The Mudiad Amddiffyn Cymru had served notice that they were still in the field.

The reasoning behind this bomb was once more connected with the Royal Family and the forthcoming Investiture…

"We knew that the Duke of Norfolk was appearing in Chester, the HQ of Western Command. The Duke was coming to address the officers of the garrison and other interested bodies who were highly involved in the organising and planning of the Investiture. After this address he was going to give a press conference. The point of our action was that for obvious reasons the Duke's coming was a closely guarded secret. The first thing that the ordinary people were to know of it was when the reporters were called in for the press conference.

"Now we knew that the Duke is a heavy drinker, and from certain accounts his tongue tends to get loose when he's taken a drop or two. We also knew that he does not like Welsh people, he has dropped this sentiment out many many times. He does not like the Welsh, apparently regarding them as a bunch of upstarts.

"The object of the exercise was to get the bomb exploded on the day he appeared in Chester. This would make him extremely annoyed because it would have shown that the security cover had been blown. Knowing his somewhat choleric temper we hoped that the bomb would have caused him to lose his cool and perhaps blurt out a sentence or two concerning his bias against the Welsh. Which would have been very useful to us as a propaganda weapon. In the event it was a reasonable success. The bomb exploded soon after 2 a.m. No one was hurt. The offices were badly damaged and there was an uproar in Chester. The barricades went up along the borders as usual, and the Special Branch went swarming into Wales.

"Naturally when the Duke appeared there was instead of peace, a bloody uproar, a total security clampdown, and people scurrying about all over the place. They realised that if he went ahead with the conference there might well be slips of the tongue, so instead of that conference they whipped him into a helicopter for an unscheduled visit to Caernarfon. Anything was preferable to letting the Duke loose with a bunch of reporters.

"The attack itself was an outside job, the bomb had been placed on a window ledge above a flat garage roof. It was only a stone's throw from the massive new police buildings, which we also had future plans for, unfortunately never to materialise …"

After this explosion Commander Jock Wilson dashed back from Scotland Yard to head the enquiries, while Chief Supt. Arthur Benfield, CID, moved with a string of detectives into Wales to follow up further enquiries. They met with little or no success, and no one was ever charged or convicted for this bombing.

Within five days the MAC struck again. This time in Cardiff where they bombed the new £731,000 police headquarters in Cathays Park. For the MAC it was to be purely symbolic, a small bomb to blow out a few windows and to demonstrate that the feared Special Branch were not invulnerable.

The chosen target area was at the rear of the building where there was an external central heating duct leading into what was thought to be the Regional Crime Squad and Special Branch offices. The Cardiff cell of the MAC was responsible for the operation, and they faced some considerable difficulties.

It could only be a small bomb because the building was occupied night and day, and the use of a block-buster would inevitably cause casualties. A major difficulty would be the actual planting of the bomb. Police complexes in Wales were tightly guarded at this period. After a lot of discussion it was finally thought best to act boldly. During the midday hours of Tuesday April 15th, two workmen wearing police-style overalls and carrying tools walked openly past the rear of the building. A quick glance showed the offices directly behind the heating duct were empty, it being the lunch hour. One workman activated the small bomb's timing mechanism, allowing the maximum twelve hours to contact point, and quickly thrust it down into the duct. The next moment he ejaculated aloud with mingled shock and fear, and bustled his companion away. The second man was resentful. "What's the matter with you?"

"Just shut your mouth and let's get from here."

"Why are you panicking?"

"You'd bloody well panic if you'd seen in there. Some fucker's planted a bloody bomb already!"

Because of the organisation's security system there was no way of reporting the fact of the other bomb back to the MAC's higher command and seeking their advice. The local leader called in his other cell members and they debated the situation. The crux of the debate was if the other object glimpsed in the duct had really been a bomb. The cell leader began to doubt the evidence of his own eyes. After all, he had only had the merest glimpse of a bomb-sized container in the shadowed duct. This operation had entailed a lot of risk. Should they now phone the police, give a warning and abort it on the strength of a suspicion? Thus making all their taken risks valueless and ensuring that there would be no chance of ever striking at the police HQ again. Tempers grew short and the argument raged back and forth, then at 4 p.m. was rendered academic by the duct blowing up. Damage was slight and no one was injured, much to the relief of the local MAC cell. But when the news of the explosion broke both they and the MAC high command were forced to recognise an unpalatable fact. Some other unknown agency was at work. Their bomb had been timed to go off at 1.30 a.m. the following day, thus minimising the risk of injury to humans. It appeared that this new, unknown bomber did not possess the same scruples as to timing, and was uncaring of causing injury to innocent bystanders.

*   *   *

The police had also taken note of this new aspect to a bombing campaign which until now had been scrupulous in its adherence to safeguarding people; and a press spokesman from the Cardiff Regional Crime Squad drew attention to the resemblance between this latest explosion and the Pembrey incident. Commander Wilson arrived in Cardiff that same evening, but despite the most strenuous and searching investigations no culprit was ever convicted.

The police were not the only force to be deeply concerned by what appeared to be an indiscriminate bomb. The MAC high command was also worried that their carefully planned campaign could be seriously damaged if anyone was killed or maimed by this unwanted escalation of extreme violence.

*   *   *

There was one ray of light in what was otherwise a gloomy landscape for the authorities. Prince Charles was now ensconced at the University of Wales in Aberystwyth for a nine weeks duration Welsh language course. There had been a few isolated examples of student rudeness concerning the Prince's stay, but the young Royal's charm and affability had soon tempered nationalist hostility upon campus. Mr Edward Millward, the one-time fire-eater who was one of the instigators of the Trefechan Bridge demonstration, appeared to have been completely won over. Mr Millward was now the Prince's personal tutor in the Welsh language at the University, and on April 21st he praised his Royal pupil's progress in that tongue most glowingly.

Not all Welshmen were won over by youthful charm however, because two days later in Left Luggage locker C10 in the booking hall at Cardiff's Queen St. railway station, a powerful bomb was found contained in a briefcase. If the bomb had exploded, which it failed to do because of faulty assembly, it could have caused havoc in the crowded booking hall. Army bomb disposal experts were called in to deal with the bomb from their temporary post in Aberystwyth, where during the Prince's stay local bomb attacks were feared. Chief Supt. David Morris, head of Cardiff's CID remarked rightly, "This was a murderous attack!"

The MAC High Command began their own immediate investigation among its cells; and caused enquiries to be made among its contacts in other extremist circles. But no one appeared to know anything about the railway station bomb. The MAC commander himself was now convinced that an independent bomber was operating, and he issued orders to all his units to keep alert for any clue as to who the unknown could be.

On Thursday April the 29th, the Central Electricity Board offices at Gabalfa was hit by another small bomb, which had been half-buried in a concrete window box, and which damaged the windows and the foyer. Night watchman Frank Hills, aged 75, was drinking tea when the bomb exploded, but had passed the explosion site only a brief time before.

Even while the last slivers of glass from this incident were being cleared, Det. Sgt. John Lavery of Abergwesyn infiltration fame and now a prosecution witness at the ongoing FWA trial, was sent a parcel bomb through the post. It had been delivered to Cathays Park police HQ, addressed personally to the Sergeant, and was received by him on May 1st. Fortunately the bomb was detected and the sergeant escaped harm. It was clear that a deliberately murderous trend was fast developing, but Chief Supt. David Morris' team had got a strong lead on the railway station bomb, and a young student at Sheffield University, Robert William Trigg, whose home address was in Cardiff, was arrested and charged with that particular offence. Although during his later trial he was to claim that the bomb had been intended as merely a hoax, he was found guilty and sentenced to five years' imprisonment.

Trigg, although a one-time member of Plaid Cymru, had

no connections at all with either the FWA or the MAC. Indeed, the latter organisation could only feel a sense of relief that such a dangerously uncontrolled operator had been removed from the scene. Mass slaughter, even by accident, was assuredly not one of their objectives as John Jenkins had repeatedly emphasised to his cell leaders…

"We could and would have had a far more intensive campaign than it was. But wherever and whenever there was the slightest risk to innocent people involved, we called the operation off. I would not countenance anyone being hurt. To kill anyone I would have to be convinced that that would be to the benefit of the coming Welsh state, or the formation of our nation. It would be the final, the ultimate conclusion that I would have to reach if there was really no other way of achieving that benefit for the state. Only then would I kill. As it was, if our bombs failed to explode at the time set, then we would make sure that the authorities were informed.

"It's strange but true that I even aided the Special Branch directly at this time to do this… A major from HQ rang me in my stores at Saighton Camp one day and asked:

'Do you think you could let some of your stuff go out of the stores for a while. Some of those dental mirrors for example?'

I demurred initially, wanting to know exactly what was happening. He said:

'Well, it's not to official sources, that is service ones. But they'll sign for everything.'

'Who are they?'

'Oh well, strictly confidential, it's the Special Branch. It's all been sanctioned by the GOC and everything.'

I then asked him what the mirrors etc. were to be used for.

'I'm very sorry,' he apologised, 'but I can't tell you. It's all very secret!'

"It was our dud bombs the dental mirrors were wanted for. You see they magnify, and by their shape enable the bomb defuser to peep around the mechanism without upsetting anything. Naturally I gave the Special Branch what they wanted, but couldn't help smiling at the irony of it as I watched them taking the stuff away.

"Of course the biggest worry for myself individually at this time were these independent bombers who could cause untold harm to us by indiscriminate bombing. Because today the battle is being fought for the hearts and minds with tactics based on psychiatrists' handbooks, and what the media makes of things. It may have something to do with force, and an ability to thumb one's nose at the authorities and get away with it. That may well start a general process of thought, which is what we were managing to do in the MAC. I was in Wrexham while we were waging our campaign and I would hear what people said about the bombs. I was in the unique position of doing something, and then hearing incognito what was said about it. I'd be in a pub or restaurant and a man would come in and say,

'I see the boys have been at it again then, ha ha ha ha ha.'

Someone would reply, 'The Special Branch say that they're on their tail and they'll have them soon.'

'Ahh, that's what they said the last time, and still they haven't got them, have they… '

"And right away there was created among the company present a sense of 'At Last'!… There seems to have been long implanted a tradition that the Welsh are very good soldiers so long as they have English officers; and that somehow a Welsh-based project never really gets off the ground… Our actions were proving these beliefs to be wrong. We were challenging the might of the police, the army and the Special Branch, and besting them. For three years they were chasing us, and even today they still have no idea of the bulk of the movement... So in one respect we had broken through on a military front. We had changed the status quo and made people wonder about the truth of the old traditions.

"I was able to hear people saying, 'Oh, another tax office has gone up now,' and they would appear highly pleased about this; and that Welshmen were striking a blow for Wales. At least, Welshmen were striking a blow for Wales, not for England... "

Chapter Twenty Eight

JUNE 1969, and as the Investiture Day drew rapidly nearer, everybody did their own thing.

Prince Charles finished his Welsh language course and left the University at Aberystwyth with the fulsome plaudits of his tutor ringing in his ears. Helicopters loaned to the police by the Ministry of Defence took to the air to mount almost continuous patrols of the water pipelines.

The militant Welsh Language Society held a rally, described here by the Patriotic Front's Keith Griffiths, then on trial at Swansea.

"… Our anti-investiture campaign had done a lot to unite militant nationalists, and Cymdeithas yr Iaith Gymraeg betrayed it by having that rally when they did. About a week before the Investiture they held a rally in Cilmeri. There we had been, focusing for months on Caernarfon, and they went to Cilmeri! When they got there they held a bloody picnic and defused the situation. 'On the way home', they told their members, 'Paint every investiture sign you see written in English, paint them out!… But not the bloody Welsh signs!' That's typical Language Society action, diffuse nationalist energy and enthusiasm by giving them pots of paint!"

Some of these pots of paint were poured over the statue of the Duke of Windsor depicting him as he was when he himself was invested as Prince of Wales. The statue, standing on the lawns before the University of Wales at Aberystwyth, had suffered indignities the previous year when two nationalists had attempted to saw its head off. At least the lavish layers of silver and green paint did not carry such overtones of the French Revolution.

There was a spate of flag burning, and bunting torn down in some Welsh towns and cities by youths; and Bethesda became noted for the continued lack of replacements to flutter along its main streets.

There was also a fear that the servicemen camping around Caernarfon for the investiture might be interfered with politically, and orders were posted to inform the Household Cavalry and others to be on their guard for subversive activities by hostile agents.

Inevitably, there were more bombs...

At 6.40 a.m. Wednesday June 25th, a floating crane operator, Mr James Crookston was waiting on Mackenzie Pier, Holyhead, Anglesey for the boat which was to take him out to the crane. A few yards away stood a plinth with a commemorative plaque, and Mr Crookston noticed a blue holdall lying against it. He examined the bag, heard a clock ticking, saw batteries and explosives inside it, and with commendable coolness ushered his work-mates away from the site and informed the police.

The CID and Special Branch acted quickly, perhaps spurred on by the words of George Thomas MP: "This was a vile act, totally detestable to the people of Wales!"

It was of course a known fact that the Royal Yacht was to be moored at the pier for one day during the Investiture period.

On June 29th, three young Welshmen, local government employees in the planning department of the Anglesey County Council were arrested in connection with the bomb. Later they were to be tried and found guilty of conspiracy and explosives charges and sentenced to imprisonment. There was a strange after-echo to this case however, following John Jenkins' own arrest...

"About Mackenzie Pier, there were three boys from Anglesey, all surnamed Jones, and they were infiltrated by an agent provocateur. They were most definitely not MAC men, despite the allegations made at their trial. They had wanted to do something for Wales, but could not find anyone belonging to us. No wonder, neither could the police. The three lads were running around making enquiries, and these came to the wrong sort of ears. They were taken in hand by this agent, who has since been identified for what he is in other cases. He gave them a drawing of what was purported to be a bomb circuitry, but also as their defence pointed out, could have been a central heating circuit. They were taken in by the police, charged, and in October 1969 sentenced for conspiracy. After my own arrest I gave evidence in their favour, which I couldn't do before, and two of them were released, but they had already served some considerable time then... "

At his own trial John Jenkins pleaded guilty to "supplying explosives for the placing by persons unknown of a time bomb at the base of a memorial plaque at Mackenzie Pier, Holyhead, with intent to cause an explosion... "

* * *

Because of the continued unrest in Wales it was obvious that the Investiture was still at risk, and equally obvious that Prince Charles himself must be given the fullest protection. The Special Branch decided to set up the biggest single surveillance operation ever mounted in Wales, to cover for the entire period of the Investiture the movements of all known Welsh extremists, a very long list. This operation would be separate from the basic security operations already ongoing and would necessitate many hundreds of additional detectives.

They were drafted into Wales from all over Britain, but in addition to these men there were considerable numbers needed to cover those known extremists living in other parts of the United Kingdom. Master-minded by Commander Jock Wilson and Mr John Parkman, *Operation Cricket* went into action. A Welsh financier, then living in London, remembers how he personally was affected by *Cricket*…

"No one was more astonished than I was when I found four members of the Special Branch sitting in front of my house. This was in London. They were very kind and gracious, and they stayed with me for about six weeks, working three shifts, two men on each shift. I had been connected with some form of nationalist movement at that time for some seventeen years, and my views were of course widely known. I appeared on the nationalist platform many times; among those who shared it with me was Elystan Morgan, then the rising star of Plaid Cymru, before he turned his coat and stood for Cardiganshire as a Labourite, and won the seat. A classic case of selling one's soul to the power system. As Junior Minister for the Home Office he as much as anyone was later instrumental in keeping the screws so harshly turned on those FWA men in prison. As the old saying goes, there is no one worse than the poacher turned bailiff.

"However, to return to *Cricket*. Although a nationalist I was not the shadowy financial figure behind the extremist movement. Perhaps I was cast in that role by one-time colleagues, hence the Special Branch surveillance. There were certain advantages to that surveillance however. It meant I could drive into town and park on double yellow lines, leave the car and go off and have a drink somewhere in the West End, safe in the knowledge that there would always be a Special Branch man by it to keep away any traffic wardens or police. The SB's would also take my children to school, and were very charming men… They tapped my phone of course, and opened my mail. What made it more interesting was at the time I was working with a government body and was giving evidence before a Select Committee in Parliament. Of course the Special Branch were not allowed to follow me into Parliament, so they had to send one of the uniformed constabulary around the building with me. You can well imagine the remarks made to me by my acquaintances among the members of Parliament when they saw me forever under escort, as it were."

Owain Williams was also under surveillance. "At the time of the investiture I was watched by the SB's for almost two months. It needed about 16 of them to cover my parents' farm, which was a large area. I remember I'd come home late at night and these two big guys would come from out of the shadows with their duffle-coats' hoods pulled over their heads. It was quite frightening you know because they were really big guys, about 6ft 2 inches average. They had their cars, usually Zodiacs or Cortinas on a special lay-by they'd built ten yards from the farm's entry lane. It was on a hill where you normally wouldn't find a lay-by, but the County Council suddenly put one there while the police were watching me. They'd be reversed into it, with their motor turning for their heater, watching me.

"At the back was another entrance which we hardly ever used. A car was stationed there. Then there were two more at different crossroads in my area. They used four two-man teams with another four teams to relieve them. They all stayed in a private hotel, Bouvian Hall. The English owner of the place told me that two of them had an old van, in the back of which was a bale of straw and a sheep. They used to go to the sales passing themselves off as dealers, but naturally were really out of place there, and looked out of place. The hotel owner said that it was the most-travelled sheep in Wales; even he laughed about it.

"The postman used to come up to the farm each day and tell me. 'You know you're being watched, don't you. There's a bloke over there with binoculars watching you, and another down by there…'

"I'd come out of the farm to fetch a loaf, the SB's would follow me. I'd go into the bakery, they'd park behind me and get a paper and read. Follow me for the rest of the shopping, back to the farm and park in the lay-by, all quite openly. My mail was opened and read, the phone was always tapped, and still is… Why even in Jubilee year a chap came here from the Post Office, he wasn't a nationalist he told me, but a Labour Party man. I'd never seen him before. He said, 'I don't like what is going on. Two men came to the office and said they wanted us to do a job for them. To put a bug in your phone. We told them to do their own dirty work. They got overalls and a Post Office van and put the bug on themselves.'

"In Llinogfawr exchange there was a little box and they had to follow the wire out. Two weeks later the same guy came to me and told me, 'Oh, it's been taken off now.'

"Quite often you can tell when the phone is tapped. You get a lot of trouble with dialling and sound. You get a double ringing of the bell as well when you're dialling out, that's a twin dial.

"During the investiture period they shoved a homing device on my car. It was a Volvo sports model, a red one. I used to do about a thousand miles a week on nationalist business, high-speed travel because the car was hotted up. They used to try and follow me. Just for spite I'd go out late at nights, down the back road with no lights on, then I'd open up. They'd hear the engine and then I'd see the lights going on everywhere, they'd be looking for me you see. Then I'd switch off on the top of a hill and watch them nearly crashing into each other as they rushed around searching for me, not knowing where I'd gone. It was quite funny…"

Not all the nationalists found surveillance amusing, and the blanket coverage by the Special Branch proved extremely effective and somewhat unnerving for those militants who had hoped to carry out some action at the ceremony itself.

The Mudiad Amddiffyn Cymru had already made its preparations for that day. But for two of their number it was to end in bloody tragedy…

Chapter Twenty Nine

IT WAS THE NIGHT of June 30th 1969, and on the morrow Prince Charles was to be invested as the Prince of Wales.

In Cardiff an unknown man pushed a small packet wrapped in brown paper through one of the post boxes fronting the Western District Sorting Office near Victoria Park. It dropped into a sorting tray and at 1.40 a.m. exploded. Six Post Office sorters had a narrow escape from injury as the rear wall of the box was shattered, and the steel-plated

It's all smiles for the cameras as Prince Charles and George Thomas enter Caernarfon Castle

front hurled into the middle of the Cowbridge Road East.

A train bearing Prince Charles and the Royal Family travelled overnight to a heavily-guarded railway siding at a secret destination in North Wales.

Thousands of police, troops and Special Branch flooded Caernarfon and its environs, checking guest lists at hotels, questioning motorists, travellers and pedestrians, and searching likely hiding places for bombs. At sea two Royal Navy minesweepers arrived in the Menai Straits. A boom was laid across the entrance to Caernarfon Harbour, and frogmen and Royal Marines in inflatable boats patrolled the shallow waters of the Seiont Estuary beneath Caernarfon Castle's walls. All along the Holyhead coastline a round-the-clock watch was maintained, for the Royal Yacht was berthed here, ready to take on board the Prince after the ceremony.

At the Castle Hotel in the small North Wales seaside town of Abergele, some 40 miles from Caernarfon two men, Alwyn Jones aged 22, and George Taylor, 37, were playing darts during the evening of the 30th. Both married men with young children, they worked for the Abergele Urban Council and were well known and popular figures in the area. They were also members of a cell of the Mudiad Amddiffyn Cymru...

At 10.40 p.m. George Taylor left the premises, and a little later with a parting joke to the landlady of the *Castle*, Alwyn Jones followed him. Just before midnight they were together in a passageway which led between Government offices off Market Street, Abergele. As they set up the gelignite bomb they had brought with them, it exploded. Alwyn Jones was blown forty yards, George Taylor died in the passageway. Both corpses were a bloodily mutilated, unrecognisable wreckage of bone and tissues. The MAC had suffered its first casualties.

* * *

Alwyn Jones

George Taylor

July 1st, and the day of the Investiture dawned dull and overcast. The ceremonies commenced with a bomb which blew up on wooded hilly ground in Love Lane, Caernarfon. The site of the explosion was only a few yards from where the Royal train was due to arrive ten minutes later, and was taken by many people to be part of the welcoming twenty-one gun salute by the artillery battery higher on the hill. No one was injured, but the security forces swarmed across the area and two young men were taken from the crowds for questioning.

The Royal train, preceded by a lone locomotive in case of landmines under the rails, drew in, and the procession through the streets was staged. Ugly incidents marred its progress. Some booing was heard and anti-investiture placards and banners waved. Eggs and banana skins were thrown at the Royal coaches by isolated individuals, on whom the loyalists in the crowd turned angrily. In most cases the police intervened quickly enough to save any serious harm being done to anyone, and many arrests were made. In one incident an estimated 500 million world-wide television viewers saw police and troops chase and apprehend a man who had been causing trouble in the Castle Square.

Numerous hoax bomb-scares were perpetrated, not only at Caernarfon but all over the Principality, and a 2000 sq. ft. marquee erected for the civic festivities at Pwllheli was deliberately burned down, and FWA slogans were again plastered across the country.

In Swansea the sentencing of the Free Wales Army commandants took place, and the court was the scene of wild commotion necessitating its clearance. Another bomb was found on the A5 trunk road near Holyhead and was defused only minutes before the Prince of Wales motorcade was due to pass the spot on its way to the Royal yacht at the port. The bomb was discovered after an anonymous telephone caller warned Mrs Catherine Griffiths that it was outside the post office where she lived.

Eight hours after the ceremony a soldier died when the army van he was sitting in beneath the Castle at Caernarfon exploded into flames. Despite the immediate suspicions of a planted bomb no evidence was ever discovered to confirm this.

The Investiture Day was inevitably claimed as a victory by both the extremists and the authorities. The extremists claimed that they had caused the ceremony to be held at gun-point, and that only 90,000, instead of the previously anticipated and hoped-for 250,000 people attended the festivities. The authorities pointed out that despite the threats of the extremists to prevent the ceremony, it had still taken place.

There was also a tragic aftermath when on July 5th 1969 a young boy, Ian Cox, on holiday with his parents went to the rear of an ironmonger's shop in Caernarfon to retrieve his ball. He saw an object and kicked it. The object exploded causing him injuries to his leg.

No one regretted this occurrence more than the MAC commander, John Jenkins, who was himself a father of small boys… "The case of the child in Caernarfon was bitterly regretted by us, and it was a pure accident. The bomb had been timed to go off in the back garden, which was on the processional route, at 2 a.m. on the morning of the Investiture. When it failed to explode at that time the usual procedure was carried out by the local cell leader. The police were phoned and informed where the bomb was. After my arrest I berated them for what I considered was their deliberate failure to act on information. The policeman's actual words when he replied were, 'Look during the week prior to the Investiture we had thousands of hoax bomb calls all over Wales. It was physically impossible to check them all out.'

"I personally was horrified when I read the first press reports of the incident, they had exaggerated the boy's injuries to such an extent. Thank God, the injuries later turned out to be much less severe than first feared.

"We, the MAC, had planned three bombs for the Investiture. The one on the hill below the artillery battery which was thought initially by both the crowd and the Television commentators to be part of the salute. One commentator actually counted the rounds aloud, and instead of 21 arrived at the total of 22; this was edited out of the final televised version. The bomb in the back garden on the processional route was the second; and a third was due to go off the following morning on Llandudno Pier. This was because the Prince was going to go from Holyhead on the Royal yacht and disembark at Llandudno Pier. It is the only mooring for a vessel that size, so if we had previously taken the pier out some hours before he was due, they would have been forced to use either a rowing boat or a coracle to bring him ashore. Which would have been an excellent propaganda victory for us... But that bomb never went off either. The police were duly notified, then sealed the Pier off and took it away, yet when I was caught they denied knowing anything about it. The story they gave me was that the dogs had smelt something, but there was nothing there. I don't know what the truth is about that.

"The Prince could easily have been killed or injured despite all the security, if this is what we had wanted. I was there at Caernarfon myself, invited as an official guest, due to some special arrangements I had previously managed to make. I personally could have very easily harmed or killed the Prince, I was so close to him at one stage of the proceedings. But apart from basic humanity, it would also not have been a good political move. The mothers of Wales would have immediately related it to the Queen, and this would have alienated them against us… Remember, we were fighting a propaganda war. It wasn't meant to kill anybody but to influence the minds of the people, and that cannot be done by taking two steps instead of one. It must be a very carefully graduated thing. You move on according to public opinion. If the movement is faster than current public opinion, then you become just another splinter group feuding with the existing state. You must always be able to claim that you are representing the wishes of the people. If you cannot, or do not do just that, then you become simply gangsters. It is imperative that you act according to the wishes of the people. Doing something on their behalf, which they want done…

"When I came home from prison it was during the great drought here in Wales. It was sweet joy to my ears to sit on buses, etc. listening to people say, 'They ought to blow the bloody lot up again! All the bloody pipelines and dams taking our water from us!' Unfortunately this reaction only happens when the man in the armchair watching television is personally bitten. If the person next door is bitten, that man doesn't mind. It's only when it bites him that he cares. Really and deeply cares… "

Vivian Davies experienced this in a bitterly-humorous way on the day of the Investiture, when he was given a suspended prison sentence and released from Swansea jail…

"When I was released from prison I jumped into a taxi and went to the council estate where I lived then at Blaen-y-maes. I was living in Dove Street, and the taxi stopped at the top of the street, He couldn't get down it, because the street was full of tables and chairs and jellies and blancmanges and flags and people laughing and singing… It really blew my mind! I'd been wanting to help lead the

Welsh people to independence and here they were, celebrating Charlie the Greek's investiture, and waving bloody Union Jacks with their mouths full of jelly! I could have wept! What can you do with people like this… ?"

Chapter Thirty

WITH THE INVESTITURE FINISHED, *Operation Cricket* could be considered a success, and later that month Commander Wilson and Mr John Parkman went to Buckingham Palace to be honoured respectively with the OBE and MBE. There was still the problem of the MAC to be dealt with however, and the Special Branch and CID now re-deployed their resources to this end.

A squad of hand-picked detectives from the Gwynedd and Cheshire forces were formed to spearhead the hunt. In charge of the team were Det. Chief Supt. Antony Clarke, head of Gwynedd CID and Det. Chief Supt. Arthur Benfield, head of Cheshire CID. Investigation in the field, concentrated in North Wales, was headed by Det. Chief Inspector William Evans and Abergele, the home town of the dead MAC members, was the focal point selected to begin with.

The police managed to establish a distinct pattern of the types of bombs used in the different incidents, but had no idea of their source. The senior officers concerned in the investigation were always wary of a possible fall-off in the enthusiasm of their men, when as the months went by despite long and arduous efforts they seemed to be getting nowhere. Particularly when another bomb was discovered at St. Martin's House, Chester, to be followed by a bomb attack on one of the main communication links between London and Northern Ireland, the South Stack Relay Station close to Holyhead, Anglesey. The security system of the Mudiad Amddiffyn Cymru was working with its customary excellence it appeared. Then, due to a momentary lapse some considerable time previously by John Jenkins, that most potent and necessary of all police aids came into the picture... an informer!

On March 1st 1968, John Jenkins had been careless... "We were going to Loggerheads near Mold, Flintshire, with the cadet band. We were going to perform the St. David's Day leek-eating ceremony in an old folks home, and after an hour's break to do the same at the delinquent children's home. In that hour's break I had arranged to meet one of my cell leaders. I was covered of course by being there with the band... Well, the orders were that no one who knew me in the organisation was ever to approach myself, or any other known member, in company with any third party. Everybody who approached must always come on their own.

"This particular fellow was very keen on a certain girl, and he brought her with him. Fair play to him, he parked the car about a hundred yards from our meeting place, then came out of it and up to me in the darkness. I got out of my car to talk to him, but because there was only a short time between this meeting and the band's next appearance I hadn't had time to change, and I was wearing full ceremonial rig. Now the point is, I wasn't wearing an ordinary uniform, but the scarlet, pre-First World War pattern of the Royal Welch Fusiliers.

"Unfortunately while we talked a car came past us, and by the momentary flash of its headlights the girl was able to see, not me as an individual, but someone wearing this rare ornamental uniform. After the Abergele tragedy this girl, knowing her friend was somehow involved in these matters, became frightened and went to the police. All she was really able to say concerning me, was that on the 1st of March, St. David's Day, 1968 she had seen her friend talking to a man wearing an unusual uniform. When the police checked in depth they found that on that night in the whole of Wales only four military had been wearing that particular uniform, myself, Alders, our Drum Major and our Goat Major. That is what caught me, it was as simple as that. The fact that one person did not fully conform to his orders. Had he come alone then they would never have found me, or at least, not unless I grew fatally careless. That girl's information made it just a simple matter of elimination for the police, and it was that moment in the car's headlights that did it. The police at my trial never called for evidence from either the girl, or the man that I had met. They didn't want evidence from them. All the police had wanted to know was who I was. A lead from which they could then get their evidence and build up their case… "

Armed with this lead from the girl, the police switched their main investigation to Wrexham. By late August they were positive that they had identified John Jenkins and Frederick Alders. In September 1969 detectives called at Saighton Army Barracks, Chester and interviewed John Jenkins. In his dental stores at the time were hidden 39 sticks of gelignite. Realising that the next visit by police would probably mean a full-scale search of the stores, and his own home, Jenkins now made his fatal error. There was no reason for supposing the Alders was in any way under suspicion, so John Jenkins temporarily handed the bomb stores over to him for safekeeping. The younger man was due to marry on the 18th October, and had rented a small cottage in Rhos to bring his new bride to. He hid the gelignite and other articles at the cottage until such time as it could be re-distributed to the various cell leaders. After the wedding, at which John Jenkins was the bridegroom's best man, the newly weds went on honeymoon, and on return settled to married bliss together with the geli.

Meanwhile the police had been feverishly collating all their available evidence and on the 2nd of November they raided the two men's homes and arrested them; in Alders' case taking something of a gamble. A search of the young man's house revealed the explosives. Under questioning Alders cracked, and after confessing his own role in the MAC, then turned Queen's Evidence against his long-time friend and colleague, John Jenkins. The older man was more saddened than made angry by this...

"Alders was a sad case. When we were taken he had only been married a fortnight. Neither of us had been in prison before and we were put into total solitary confinement in Shrewsbury. Not seeing anyone at all, and only coming out of our cells for a period of exercise. We, of course, never glimpsed each other. A doctor was coming round every day to check our mental and physical health. I was alright, but Alders was in a bad way. It broke him in the end. I'm sorry he turned Queen's Evidence naturally, but I feel no bitterness towards him, that's the way life is... "

On Monday, April 20th 1970, John Barnard Jenkins, aged 37, was jailed for ten years for eight offences involving explosives. Throughout his trial and subsequent imprisonment he refused to name or implicate any other member of the organisation.

Frederick Ernest Alders, aged 22, was sentenced to six years' imprisonment after admitting charges concerned with explosives. He was released long before this period had elapsed.

With the loss of their brilliant commander the Mudiad Amddiffyn Cymru ceased active operations, and the first Welsh rebellion since the days of Owain Glyndwr was finally defeated.

The last actual explosion caused by the MAC came on the 5th November 1969, three days after John Jenkins' arrest.

The cell leader in Anglesey took the gelignite remaining from the South Stack explosion, and detonated it on wasteland, thus igniting the biggest banger of Guy Fawkes Night…

John Jenkins after his release in 1976

Chapter Thirty One

DECADES HAVE PASSED since the events described in this story. Many of the principal protagonists still live in Wales. Older, perhaps wiser, they look back on their years as rebels with a sense of nostalgia, tempered with regret and some bitterness. After all, despite their failure to achieve their aims, they did experience headily-exciting days, very different from the dullness of ordinary routine existence; and Rebellion is a rich and potently intoxicating draught for those who taste it…

The question could be asked, will armed rebellion ever erupt in the Wales of the future?

At the Cilmeri Stone in December 1978 on the anniversary of the death of Prince Llewelyn, a solemn torchlit ceremony took place. Among the wreaths laid upon the Stone was one bearing the emblem of the White Eagle of Snowdon. Beneath its crest were inscribed the words…

"FE GODWN NI ETO" — WE SHALL RISE AGAIN.

The End

A Tribute to Cayo
by Dafydd Gwyn

4th of April 1995, on the day of his funeral

William Edward Julian Cayo Evans (22-4-37 to 29-3-95)

Cayo was my friend, and I loved him.

It is a greater honour than all worldly riches – and a far greater honour than those awarded by states and governments – that I should be asked by the family to make this address.

I shall try to proclaim it as a worthy eulogy.

Cayo was a great man – remember him

I do not have the skill and art to do justice to my task. I am certain that poetry will be written in his memory; elegies that will compare with those of our Welsh Princes. Poems that will forever strengthen his rôle in the history and conscience of Wales.

Cayo was a brave hero. His life and deeds will not have been in vain.

He stands with Saunders Lewis as a twentieth Century icon of the Welsh Nation. I believe that posterity will establish him as one of the Nation's foremost champions.

Cayo had a vision – remember him

History will establish Cayo as a legendary figure.

Future generations will remember and act on his vision. He had a vision of a free Wales. "To Dream of Freedom" – what an apt title of a book already written about him and his comrades-in-arms.

He spoke of his dream – summoning his people to build anew a Nation's pride. He spoke out against the injustice of foreign domination, despoilment and treachery.

Cayo had a vision – remember him

It is significant that he united Wales from Môn to Merthyr, from Llanelli to Llandudno – receiving as much support, if not more, from the anglicised communities as from the Welsh-speaking heartlands. He was chieftain of many clans. His leadership was unique.

Cayo had a vision – remember him

We Welsh pride ourselves on being a classless society. Cayo embodied that belief. Without effort, he was the same to all, from whatever background, in whatever circumstance.

He was a fine-natured gentleman.

He did not flaunt his education and erudition, but with brilliant flashes of insight made every meeting with him memorable.

Cayo was a natural aristocrat. He was respected by his enemies and those who were in conflict with him. Cayo had charisma.

Cayo had a vision – remember him

Let us be mindful that there is nothing but pity for those who deride when a great man stumbles – or when the man of action could have done better.

All credit must go to the doer of deeds who has striven valiantly. Cayo lived the great enthusiasms; Cayo knew the triumph of high achievement; Cayo knew the failures, but at least in failing, did so whilst daring greatly, so that his place will never be with those poor and timid souls who know neither victory nor defeat.

Cayo had the passion, intelligence and emotional strength to stand far above his critics.

Cayo had a vision – remember him

Recently an English commentator stated that Cayo and what he stood for would only be "a footnote in history". That will not be so.

Those who pay tribute throughout the whole of Wales will not let it happen. His life, his endeavours, his daring, his gallantry, his greatness will not have been in vain. Harri Webb's verses are fitting:

Far heard and faintly calling
Held between hill and hill,
Echo on echo falling
The thunder lingers still.

The highborn and the lowly
In their great love overthrown
For the earth that is more than holy,
For the land that is ours alone.

And by ways that are wonder and mystery
From silence and shadow they come
From memory and legend and history
They arise to the beat of the drum,

The heartbeat that hammers with longing
In the breasts of the few who are brave
That summons the heroes thronging
From the gallows and the grave.

And the sunrise shall not blind them
Who bestir to the last alarm
To the host that rallies behind them
And lends its strength to their arm.

Cayo will be among those heroes – a commander, a chief.

Cayo had a vision – remember him

* * *

Let the whole Nation cherish his memory as he reposes in the company of the warriors who have fought for Cymru's freedom.

He would not wish us to mourn his passing in sorrow. Let us all feel proud that we knew him. He would wish all of us to rekindle our passion, and to redouble our efforts to make his vision reality.

God bless his great soul. May God bless and keep his beloved children Siân Dalis and Rhodri Owain, and his dearest Delyth. May their faith console and keep them in their grief.

Also published by Y Lolfa:

A new look at the fight for independence

GWYNFOR EVANS

The Fight for Welsh Freedom

y Lolfa

£6.95

ISBN: 0 86243 515 3